MW00643219

Three
Wild Dogs

(and the truth)

Also by Markus Zusak

The Underdog
Fighting Ruben Wolfe
When Dogs Cry
I Am the Messenger
The Book Thief
Bridge of Clay

Three
Wild Dogs

(and the truth)

A Memoir

Markus Zusak

HARPER

An Imprint of HarperCollins*Publishers*

THREE WILD DOGS (AND THE TRUTH). Copyright © 2024 by Markus Zusak. All rights reserved. Printed in the United States of America. No part of this book may be used or reproduced in any manner whatsoever without written permission except in the case of brief quotations embodied in critical articles and reviews. For information, address HarperCollins Publishers, 195 Broadway, New York, NY 10007.

HarperCollins books may be purchased for educational, business, or sales promotional use. For information, please email the Special Markets Department at SPsales@harpercollins.com.

Originally published in Australia in 2024 by Pan Macmillan Australia Pty Ltd.

FIRST U.S. EDITION

Illustrations by Daniel New
All photographs courtesy of the author unless otherwise noted.

Library of Congress Cataloging-in-Publication Data has been applied for.

ISBN 978-0-06-342607-8

24 25 26 27 28 LBC 5 4 3 2 1

For Halina Drwecka
and
in loving memory of Jacek –
we miss you

Three
Wild Dogs

(and the truth)

prologue

THE WILDERNESS WITHIN

There's nothing like having a punch-up with your dog on a crowded city street:

The intersection is vast.

The oncoming judgment, electric.

In a way it's almost a relief, as I gather my thoughts and fortitude. I've had moments with dogs before (moments you might not believe), and I can smell when there's one in the making.

To quickly describe the neighborhood, it's shockingly, awfully affluent, but there's plenty of rubbish on the ground. It's Sydney's eastern suburbs, and there are something like nine lanes of cars. It's one of the bigger, more bustling traffic points, of Ocean Street, Syd Einfeld Drive, Oxford, a veering left onto Wallis, and the Woollahra Gates of Centennial Park. There are turning lanes, street crossings, pedestrians. There are cyclists and all manner of people, and people with all manner of dogs. And almost, always, *Cavoodles*.

The dog I will fight is Frosty.

Frosty is *not* a Cavoodle.

He's a big, white, boisterous, wiry-furred pound dog – probably a version of wolfhound cross – with a black nose, pink skin and snout, a smattering of spots on his ears, and a rancorously happy smile. He has two big brown patches on his backside, like a baboon, or the exact same shape that The Artist Formerly Known as Prince used to cut – for some permanently bewildering reason – into the rump of some of his outfits. (When people see those patches, they either laugh or suggest what the dog might have sat in, which we like to take in our stride.)

There was conjecture about Frosty's name when we bailed him out of the group home.

A few points on that last sentence:

First, my wife wanted to rename him Ziggy. Full name Ziggy Frost. Our kids were keeping it simple. The name on the Sydney Dogs and Cats Home website was Frosty, and they were more than willing to fight for it.

Second, I've never been able to say *rescue center*, or call any of my dogs a rescue. I remember a David Sedaris story where he mocks the self-righteous dog owner type, who loves bragging that his or her dog is exactly that – a rescue. I discovered the story long after we'd taken in our wild, ferocious, temperaments-only-a-mother-could-love pound dogs (Frosty is the third – the other two have since departed this world), but he hit the nail on the head. We're not special for taking in these 100 percent nonpedigrees – we're idiots. Okay, we're idiots *and* we're right. Some poor half-breed Staffy or Kelpie is just sitting there panting in his prison cell, waiting for either the final injection (as my mum always calls it) or a bleeding-hearted dilettante to come along and say, 'That's the one, Agnes! *That's the one,*' totally ignorant of the chaos to come. Or worse, completely attuned to it, but unable in the end to resist.

So at our place we call it like it is.

Our dogs have come from the pound.

But recently I've taken it further.

The pound has become the *group home.*

'Shit,' I'll shout, 'bloody Frosty! If he does that one more time, I'm sending him back to the group home!'

Mika, my wife: 'What's he done *this* time?'

'Oh, just the usual, I can't even put my shoes on. He keeps headbutting me!'

'And jumping on you?'

'Yeah.'

'And clawing you?'

'Yeah!'

'Oh my God, what a pain in the arse!'

'*Yeah!*'

But it's amazing how all this is spoken. There are smiles on faces, laughter on stairs. He's just desperate for a walk, after all. It was clear he never got out much before. In the first few months we had him, it was like walking a rolling thunderstorm. Or ADHD on legs. But more of that to come.

For now, I should quickly expand on what I was saying earlier, to clean it all up properly, from the start – like when you go to a public event, and they tell you about the house-keeping. Turn your phone to silent, and so on.

Here, the housekeeping is different. You should know, or be warned, what's coming. It's mostly the termi-nology – or the rudeness, gruffness, and maybe just downright hostility. I mean, I'm supposed to be a nice guy. I'm friendly, I'm a good person. I'm known to be easygoing, and generous of spirit. But when you start to write about your life, as opposed to writing fiction (which I normally do for a living), you can take a few different directions. You can either project what people think of you, and be polite and winning, and right. Or you can show people who you *really* are. Impatient, annoyed, foul-mouthed, sometimes cruel. In constant battle to be your better self, but never quite getting close . . . especially while being trodden on by a big white dog in the hallway.

Case in point?

The *group home.*

Is it insensitive to call the dog rescue center, or pound, a group home? Is it callous toward, or unfeeling of, people who've been in that situation, or might be in it even as we speak? Is there a chance I don't care at all? I'll leave that for you to judge.

What I *will* say is that I haven't necessarily been the model citizen people think I am, or should be, especially in terms of my dogs. I've done some pretty unconscionable things.

There have been murders, for example, and cover-ups. (I promise, I can explain.) There have been street fights, park fights, an array of more casual beatdowns, and vandalism, mostly at home. There's also been a lot of swearing, cursing and blasphemy. There's been name-calling, shaming, shit-talking, erupting, grudge-making (and holding) – the lot. The police were called once because one of our neighbors thought a dead body was being hauled singlehandedly through our backyard by Mika, at two o'clock in the morning. We've had dogs getting their stomachs pumped, I've been knocked out cold in the grass. I've tackled a tall goddamn *supermodel* of a dog, somewhere in the dark of night, calling him every name you can think of. I've lied, I've cheated. I've lashed out, I've barked.

But also, and this might be my one saving grace.

For whatever reason –

I've loved.

We are entering my life as a dog.

Which brings us back to Frosty, or the Frost, or just plain Frost.

(We're constant shorteners, lengtheners and nicknamers at our place, and Frosty is no exception. He already has a good parade of alternative names, ranging from Buddy, Bud, Shithead, Baby, Tufty, Chubby Cheeks, Boxhead, Mush Mouth, Whitey, Snowy, Frostel, Frozballs, Frozman, Frozzle, Frozzy – and right from the very start, the standard Eastern European handles that come easily to families with names like Zusak. Things like Frostusczko, Frostusch, Frostolusch, Frosthund, and so on . . .)

Either way, whatever the combination of names, on any given day, Frosty's the last piece of the puzzle – the trigger to get things written.

To put that into some kind of perspective, people have been telling me I should write about my dogs for the better part of a decade. As someone who normally blends into the background when out in public, or isn't noticed at all, I've been recognized, many times, because of those hounds. Those lumps of fur and panting. They've been such a big part of my life.

The problem, however, has been this – when it came to writing about them, there was always something missing. There are so many books inside us, it seems, but they mostly remain unready. They're dormant, untold mountains. Volcanoes without a top. There are plenty of fires within the place, just not the one to set it all off. In the case of my life with these animals, it's only now I've found the way. What I needed was the third dog in. A conduit back to the past.

For this book, I thank the Frost.

His predecessors were Reuben and Archer:

Gangsters, gunmen. Soldiers.

They lived and frightened together.

Essentially a two-dog mafia.

Their intimidation became quite legendary, but there were maps to hearts of gold. Reuben was a godless philistine, but capable of giant love. Archer was really quite elegant – he could be the perfect gentleman. Given the appropriate circumstance.

First Reuben died – a fallen, hardened warrior, after a Johnny Cash–sized life. Then Archer went soon after, like a tide just swept him up somehow and carried him all the way out.

A dying dog is precious.

Forget diamonds, pearls and any other worldly treasures. Give me fur and stink and pleading eyes, and the sad warm dog in your arms. You can't know how much you loved them, I think, till you call for the executioner, or you get the results from the blood tests, and just stand in the shower and cry.

For a while after each of them left us, I attempted to write their lives. I couldn't get further than a page or two. Usually, I know if I can write a book by the end of the very first sentence. But it can take an age to find it.

For the most part, it was perfectly normal.

I realized it wasn't quite time.

Book ideas almost never work to begin with. I often describe the project I'm working on as a world that exists beside me. I know it's going well when I feel like I can roll out of bed in the morning and land *there*, inside the book. But it's a little bit like respect – hardest thing to get, easiest thing to lose.

That said, these dog stories were meant to be simple. They were raw and recent, and near. Their truth was both stranger and badder than fiction. So what was it that kept me from writing them?

There were so many starting-off points, to launch a thousand stories – of wild and lawless mornings, and dog day afternoons. They'd been in then out of my life, between 2009 and 2021, but for some reason I couldn't find traction. Maybe there was just too much of them. Too much mass destruction. Too many awkward tragedies. And, of course, too much sheer, unadulterated comedy. After all, what do you get a dog for if not for the chaos itself – to ask anarchy straight to your door? We all seem to covet control of our lives, but we unravel it with reckless abandon. We have children, we take in animals. We agree to more work than we should. We coach an unruly football team.

For me it's been many, or actually, all of those things, but the clincher was Reuben and Archer:

A life with a wild pair of dogs.

Looking back, I can only smile, though, for they were dogs who somehow made me, or at the very least, remodeled. They were a mirror, I suspect, to my own hidden turmoils – my wilderness within. In a way they charted time, and often, I'll even say to people, especially dog owners who don't have children: 'When you think about it, it's not a

7

bad way to live – to remember your life by your dogs.' (I can usually measure what year something happened, purely by the dog in the picture.)

To be honest, time was often at the forefront when it came to Reuben and Archer; I was forever looking to outlast.

Further to earlier descriptions (and maybe police mug shot photos), Reuben was a big bad brindle thing, like a wolf at your door with a hacksaw – a dark prince in exile, or purgatory. Then Archie was a pretty boy assassin – a handsome blond with honey-gold eyes, and legs with a lineage to royalty, or at the very least, Grace Kelly. Which was always the hazardous irony, for it was him we really looked out for. We were sure he was Reuben's hitman.

It's one of those things you hate to admit, maybe like a problem with alcohol: *I'm an owner of dangerous dogs.*

At some point I adopted a mantra.

All I have to do, I'd think, *is get these two dogs through. Just get them through their lives without them seriously hurting someone* – they were a clear-cut hazard to humans at times – and truth be told, I did. Well, at least when it came to the community. No injuries required hospitalization. (Of course, an ambulance was called once for *me*, and years later I needed surgery.) But there were definite scrapes and stitches, and certain incidents led to notoriety. One of your dogs biting a piano teacher, for instance, is nothing if not exciting. It gives people plenty to talk about, as you fall to new depths of shame. Oh, God, the awful infamy!

But enough.

My final points.

*

Initially, it was losing Reuben.

Not long after he died, and it was typical of that dog – a death of brutal beauty – Mika appeared one night and spoke to me. 'I really think you should write about him.'

I tried, but I couldn't feel anything.

Then with Archer I was just too broken.

What it took was a period of waiting, then the arrival of a new impostor, as they all are in the beginning – not quite yet themselves, and never to be quite *them*: shaping up to the dogs of our memory. What came in was a blast from the cold.

We always said that when all our animals died (we had two cats as well), we'd have a gap year before even considering. There were delusions of grandeur like this one: 'We'll finally be able to travel! We can live in New York for three months, then Barcelona, then anywhere else we want . . .'

But when all the animals were gone, it was 2021. The COVID ward of the world. There was nowhere to go in the country, let alone beyond, and there were dogs in want of a home. When Archer died, on April 20 of that year, the plan was to wait six months, at least. We needed the pain and sadness. To be alone, to be without. But we also welcomed the break.

Six months.

We lasted three.

Our children were more than ready by then. (Kids who know animals are canny. Ours aren't ones to pester; they mentioned it once, then waited.) Privately, I'd already made the mistake of seeing dogs peering out of computer screens, but none of them felt quite right, till I saw this dope called Frosty. I couldn't know what a gift he would give me – the perfect start I needed, in a very public setting:

A man at war with his dog.

*

Imagine what it looks and sounds like now.

The sunset sun of Sydney.

It's somewhere near end of August, half-past five in the evening, the light swelling the way it does here – engorged till finally dying – then bronze behind the buildings. We're still in the grip of pandemic mode, which means more people on the street than ever, and a multitude walking their dogs. (Say what you want about Sydneysiders, but the best way to get us out exercising is to tell us we can't go outside.) There's traffic despite the lockdown, all cars and their drivers and music. There are people in jackets, dogs on leashes, and my pulse grown warmer inside me. It beats from my neck to my feet.

We're coming back out of the park, where the Frost has just had the time of his life – *the absolute greatest time* – but this is where it all gets heavy, because now he's back on the leash, which gathers immediate meaning:

FROST ON LEASH = MANIC

It was something we knew, almost from minute one.

There would be violence out on the streets.

You see, somewhere inside him, Frosty knows. He has to make it to every last dog he lays eyes on, and he has to get to them *now*.

Does he want to hurt them?

No. He doesn't.

What he wants to do is hurt *us*.

To get to those dogs and play with them, talk to them, run with them, he'll butcher our legs and knees. He'll hoist himself in any direction he can, before mauling again at our quadriceps. There are teeth on flesh and cartilage. He wants us out of the way.

Sure, we'd done our best with him. When you've spent a decent portion of your life managing a pair of threatening dogs, you're lulled into a sense of security. You think you can handle anything. And then you bring in a new one.

We'd tried securing him with treats. It didn't work. I'd kept him on the tightest rein. Again, predominant failure. The firm, taciturn teacher's voice? It meant nothing to Group Home Frosty. He knew how to win what he wanted.

For close to two months at that point, we'd been afraid to encounter any other dog on the street. He would gain momentum in centimeters and attack us from the side. Poor Mika had a crossbreed of bruises around her knees – black, then blue, and yellow.

Till eventually, I decided to *decide*.

I would do what had to be done, and what you might well choose to hate me for. I would open that secret within, to the blood and the heat of the wilderness – to answer all he was asking. Was I the boss, or was he?

The next time he tried to go through me?

I was going to go through *him*.

It's interesting when you're standing there, waiting for the lights to change. You count the opposing humans, you account for their arsenal of dogs – and by that I mean their *innocuous* dogs, inciting war by merely existing. There's the little digital figure, red but soon to be green. Then me and the frost-colored wild thing.

The transition is made, the chattering computerized sound begins – a call to the oncoming animals.

One step, and immediately he's launched at me, and what can I say but this? Hell hath no fury like a man whose dog's been attacking him, who's decided to fight him back. Worst of all, we're completely surrounded by this horde of normal people. Normal people with uncrazy dogs.

Me, I'm trading blows with Frosty, and to be honest, he's in some shock. *Bang.* Open hand. Then another one, at his first attempt at a comeback – my palm against his snout. Was that an uppercut or a hook? It doesn't matter, because now he's pinned to the ground, while people are passing by, and my voice, curled tight, against him. '*You will never – EVER – do that to me again! EVER! Do you hear?!*'

Wide-eyed, he's staring up at me.

He's sideways, slapped to the concrete.

Breathing heavily.

Both of us.

Is that the slightest suggestion of a nod?

The people walking by, they watch and I just don't care. I almost want them to say something, but I'm also thinking, Nothing to see here, just keep going. And no one says a word. This is Sydney after all. Judgment hurled in silence.

Of course, when Frosty's allowed back up, we still have one more crisis – and I use that word discriminately, for this is more than just a problem.

Our chance to cross is over.

We have to wait here again, and wait here again we will, till we get this to work how it should. How hard can it possibly be to cross these lanes of traffic? In the moment it's disgrace and adrenaline, but now, looking back, I see it. I see what fills that space between, to the distant shore of *making it*.

It's the time gone by with dogs, I think, and everything that comes along with it. Even the common platitudes, like we don't really get to choose our dogs, or rescue them, but it's them who rescue us.

Which is true, but also bullshit.

When it all comes down to it, it's work. It's work, and a lot of it's dirty work. They change our lives for the messier, but the mess is outrageously memorable – and really, what more can we ask for? There's not a dog I want to forget.

So now it's come down to this.

Again, the lights will change.

A whole new crowd of people will have gathered with their spaniels, retrievers and lapdogs. Grudgingly, I'll watch them accumulate.

Yes, all we have to do is traverse this road, and its many temptations and perils. There's a madman dog beside me, and the hounds of memory ahead of us – all in our pages to come. It's love and beasts and wild mistakes, and regret, but never to change things.

We plunge, dog-first, to the maelstrom.

part one

REUBEN

THE CLIMBED-OUT DOG FROM
THE GROUND

What's strange is we start with cats.

We had two.

They were tabbies, run of the mill, although one was especially beautiful, with great green eyes and a patch of white, like a vest down the front of his chest. The other was heavier, more working-class. Bulkier stripes of gray, and big black tarmac paws.

The prettier one was named Bijoux, by Mika.

The heavier one was Brutus, named by me.

Without any shadow of a doubt, we would class ourselves as animal people, and within that, our subgroup is dog people, so how we started with cats is a mystery.

It was 2003.

We lived in a small townhouse in the south of Sydney.

(Maybe that was why we opted for cats, although other people in the complex had dogs.)

Our first ports of call were the closest animal shelters

and a few other refuge sites, but there were no cats available at all, so we bought them from the local pet shop. Mika picked out Bijoux from a dozen or so cats in a cage. Four or five weeks later, Brutus was the only one left. He was too big to be cute enough anymore, not kitten-worthy, and the shop owner offered him to us for free. 'Best cat I've ever had here,' he said, and we were more than willing to believe him. There were no cardboard boxes and they were closing up, so Mika carried him home – where he was beaten from pillar to post. Bijoux, it turned out, was relentless.

Of course, it's fair if you're wondering why a book about a writer and his dogs might begin with two gray kittens, but believe me, those cats were essential warm-ups:

Bijoux was a warrior. A feline Genghis Khan.

Brutus, the eternal softie.

(Although, years later, we did see him bring a dead rat in one night and eat the whole thing in the corner of our bedroom. Honestly, he just tucked in like he was in some kind of mess hall. It conjured up all those movies you see, of corporals at basic training, really shoveling their food down. I can still hear Mika's voice, hauling me out of sleep.

'Kochanie, Brutus has brought in a rat – oh no, that's bad, that's terrible – OH! Holy shit, he's eating it!'

Like statues we sat and watched him.

Perennial pillars of salt.

'He's not gonna eat the tail, is he?'

Don't-look-don't-look-don't-look.

'Oh no, I think he's going to.'

That tail was gone in a heartbeat.

The rat had completely vanished.

But still, I have to be truthful here, I acknowledged the silver lining; I was glad I didn't have to dispose of it. Those jobs always fell to me, and this time the work was done. Just the carpet and a few spots of blood.)

Now, I know that's pretty barbaric, but Brutus – more commonly known as Brutie – really was the more sensitive of the two. He had a high-pitched, almost silent method of meowing, but he purred louder than your average vacuum. He made himself comfortable on your lap in the living room, or at your desk, or on the bed, and he'd curl himself into a tortoiseshell.

Bijoux, as I've said, was the menacing one. He scratched you to wake you up, normally on your face – or on toes or feet left exposed. He had mega-fights with neighboring cats and won with pitiless ease, despite his diminutive size. When he meowed, he threw his whole body into it. You would hear it and think, Man, that cat is *pissed off.* Even years later, when I'd say things like, 'We've got two cats, two dogs and two children – and the children are the easiest,' it was Bijoux I was referring to most. I would go away to a writers' festival, or on a book tour, and I'd wonder why things were so quiet. It wasn't screaming kids or barking dogs I was missing, but the ferocity of Bijoux's meowing. Every single word from that cat's mouth, from morning to night, was a litany of planned profanity. We knew exactly what he was saying.

Six a.m., he'd confront you:

– HOW ABOUT SOME BLOODY *FOOD, SHIT*HEAD?! WHAT ARE WE WAITING FOR – CHRISTMAS? SHIT!

And so on.

Eight o'clock, ten o'clock, midday, afternoon, it was

basically an all-day affair. He treated humans like we were target practice. While Brutus rested – purring somewhere, most often on my open laptop – Bijoux lay in wait like a sergeant.

— YOU AGAIN! he would bark. (I know, I know, but let's go with it.) — ARE YOU AWARE THERE'S NO MORE DRY FOOD?! GET ON IT, *SHIT-FOR-BRAINS*!

Honestly, there were times I could have strangled him, but there was also a measure of respect. He was tough, I'll give him that much. He might have looked like a private school boy, but his heart pumped the blood of a thug. Had he lived by a code or belief system, I'm sure it was pure and simple: *I don't take nothin' from no one.*

We're confident Bijoux burned through many more than his nine lives, too, till he finally went out on his sword – a story for later, it's a big one.

In those early years, he fell at least twice from a three-story height and walked away like nothing had happened. He survived the meanest spate of paralysis ticks we'd ever seen. At one point, his head was jammed between two giant rocks, hidden among some bushland, probably for a solid thirty-six hours. The list goes on and on.

(An afterthought now, in my edits: he *could* also be very sweet, that cat, in a dynamic or visceral way. If he loved you, he loved you hard. He purred with physicality. He rubbed deftly against your shins, interlocking himself at your feet. His tail, a wandering cobra. He knitted happy-paws on your lap before settling down for hours. I remember those parts as well, but his rough stuff was so extreme, and therefore much easier to document.)

*

The best example of Bijoux's toughness, though, was a memorable Saturday morning, and not a claw was lifted in violence. It was the standoff out on the driveway.

Not long after we bought the cats, we moved to a place a few kilometers away. It was a cedar house on stilts, on a big steep block in what you might call the backwaters of Sydney. We were hidden down a hill, behind some other houses. There were retaining walls of various heights, and vacant blocks either side of us. Maybe fifty meters south, our closest neighbors also had a cat: a behemoth prowler called Jackson. And Jackson had made some bad calls in life, one of which he was soon to rethink.

Essentially, for a good few months after we moved in, he was routinely entering through our cat flap and pilfering Bijoux's dry food. (I say *Bijoux's* because he was probably renting out the few bits and pieces he didn't want anymore to Brutie.) Sometimes we'd walk into the laundry and there was the burglarious Jackson – a giant, brooding presence. He was white with a patchwork of black, hunched at the bowl, gorging his gluttonous heart out on dry Snappy Tom or Whiskas. Till one thing became quite certain:

Bijoux had decided to *decide*.

Outside, near our laundry door and the flap, was a last little slab of retaining wall. Sandy-colored, nice geometry. It was barely a few feet high.

We were going out to the shops, and as we came by the side of the house, we saw the peculiar sight. On top of that wall, Jackson and Bijoux were engaged in psychological warfare. Both were crouching forward, utterly still, nose to nose. The best way to describe it is like a carbon copy of a promotional boxing poster I once had – *Ali vs. Frazier II* – where the fighters fiercely eye each other, a millimeter from actually touching.

'Hey, Mika,' I said, 'look at that.'

Neither cat moved a muscle. Not a whisker, not a tendon. Knowing Bijoux like we did, we were fairly sure of what he was saying, too, to Jackson the greedy embezzler.

— Lemme just tell you one – thing – *fat*boy. This is a line you no longer cross. Move one step closer and I'll take your goddamn retinas out. I'll eat your neat little ears off – *got it?*

Three hours later, we returned.

Both cats were as they were.

Neither had given ground, but as far as we could tell, Jackson never came back.

So that was the life we were living.

Mika, me, a pair of cats, in a house on stilts in the suburbs.

In 2006, we had a daughter and named her Nikita. For a while she was shortened to Niki, but she soon decided on Kitty. She was three years old when Mika had itchy feet, ready again to move house. (In those days she liked to move once every three or four years. Now it's different, she stays and renovates.) The best part of that story for me was that I'd told people repeatedly that I loved this house so much they'd need to carry me out of it in a box. These days, I acknowledge it was the right time to move, but I still look back very happily. We had a lot of beautiful times in that house. We laughed a lot. I wrote my most successful book there. But, tellingly, it's that image I'll remember forever, of Jackson and Bijoux, eye to eye, on that wall. Even now, with Bijoux gone – and I'm sure

Jackson, too – I see them there in spirit, neither giving ground in the afterlife.

In September, 2009, we moved to where we live now.

We don't belong in the eastern suburbs, not really – one of the fancier parts of Sydney.

Mika's from the west.

I'm from the distant south.

The house we bought here was old and beautiful, in need of a bit of work, with an abnormally big backyard for a block so close to the city center. We joked that we would bring local property values down with the worn-out old car I couldn't let go of, and the fact that I threw up on the street when I caught a twenty-four-hour bug not even a week after moving in. On top of that, we had two base-quality cats – and soon, a mangy dog.

Talk of a dog started because Kitty loved all animals, but she especially gravitated to dogs. Mika's mum and dad had two, both of the big-dog variety, and Kitty was taught to respect them. She hugged them, she treasured them, but she never crossed the line. She would never be climbing on their backs, or mashing up their faces, and the dogs loved her in return.

Earlier that year, about four months before we moved, we'd visited our friends, Dana and Daniel, and their daughters, in San Francisco. I'd met Dana in 2006, on my first-ever book tour, which turned out to be in America, for that book I'd written in our previous home. It was a novel I thought would fail, called *The Book Thief*. Unlike most book tours, which are set up by publishers to be taken alone, it was a group of authors all traveling together, and many of us became great friends. There was Dana Reinhardt, then the excellent husband-and-wife writers Laura and Tom McNeal, and me.

(The McNeals live in San Diego. Back then they had a sweetheart Doberman named Edna – the most beautiful sook in the world. Even in San Diego's constant warmth and comfort, she would stand at the back door and shiver; her ploy to be indoors with the rest of us.)

As for our stay in San Francisco, Dana's dog was Chayo – a golden mix of Collie, I think, whom she and Daniel had found totally neglected on the streets in Boston. They picked her up and drove her home, and I love the story of that drive – how they'd found this beautiful, malnourished dog, then got impatient with her in the car. Chayo started whining from about the time they hit New Mexico, then all the way to California.

'Chayo, Jesus, shut *up!*'

Then, of course, they'd started feeling guilty.

It was the first of many inklings that love isn't always patient. Especially when it comes to dogs.

It was Dana who came out and said it one afternoon.

'You need to get Kitty a Chayo.'

It's the sort of thing she would rattle off quite bluntly, while we sat on the front steps of her house. Kitty would be gently hugging the dog, telling her about her day. Chayo listened thoughtfully. Dana, her shortish blond hair. Jeans and shirt, black puffer vest. There's always a chill in San Francisco. She would rub her hands and go, *'Brr.'* Kitty continued patting, and narrating, and Dana turned toward us.

'You know I'm right, right?'

We did.

The doubt really only set in once we were home.

Months passed, we moved to this old house, and in November, it was late, I was working. Usually I don't work very late, I'm an early riser, but sometimes I'll make a start in the evening.

At the time, Mika had a desk set up in our bedroom. (She's the other half of our writing business, managing and balancing the books.) I was in the room across the hall when her voice carried through.

'Hey, I think I found us a dog.'

I looked up. I looked away.

The book I was working on was *Bridge of Clay*, and I was feeling its darkening waters. I'd finished writing *The Book Thief* in August 2004, so it had been five years already since I'd got something done, and I was still wrestling with the first few chapters. More troubling than that, I was constantly revisiting the first page – and worse again, the opening *sentence*. (Quite tellingly, *Bridge of Clay* was eventually finished by the end of 2017. Thirteen years in the writing.)

On top of that not entirely small problem, there were other factors to consider.

First, another child was well on his way.

Second, one of the truly special outcomes of moving was that the cats were routinely marking their territory inside, though it was difficult to work out where – which always reminds me of the people you tell this to, and their advice is something like, 'Well, you just have to get rid of them.'

I would look at those people and say, 'What am I, a crime lord? Should I throw them in the harbor, tied to a block of concrete?'

Third, despite *The Book Thief* becoming that lucky kind of success any writer dreams of, we'd borrowed a lot of money to buy this house. We still had bills to pay and a three-year-old daughter to wrangle. Yes, she loved animals and had a beautiful heart, but she could still be a tough little hombre. I wondered if throwing a dog into the mix right now was exactly what we needed.

But sometimes, we just have to go there.

No one is really exempt.

We decide to make the mistake.

I stood up from my desk.

I could see Mika from the corner of my eye, but I didn't go in and talk to her. Instead, I walked to the window.

Like most of us, one of the first metaphors I ever learned was *It's raining cats and dogs* . . . But what if there's an almighty cyclone, and it delivers only a single dog, like an animal flung to Earth? Or what if the deluge washes a mountain away, and a dog climbs out of the ground?

That, in a sense, was Reuben.

An almost mythical creation.

It was in my hands, but out of them.

'What was that?' I finally answered. 'Did you just call out to me a minute ago? Something about a . . . ?' I could taste the word *dog* in my mouth, but couldn't quite commit to releasing it.

And it's one of the things with Mika, I think.

I could almost *hear* her smiling.

She grinned, she said, 'You heard me.'

A KNACK FOR FINDING
PROBLEM DOGS

That night in November 2009, Mika was scanning the internet for abandoned dogs. My obvious advice for anyone approaching those animal websites is that whatever you do, if you're only fifty percent sure, don't look. Once you've looked, you're gone. You might as well start buying the food, the leashes, the beds, the toys, and finding your nearest vet. The more intelligent among you might also start looking up pet insurance.

When Mika called out that she'd found us a dog, the dilemma was immediately twofold. First, God love her as I do, she's good at knowing what she wants. Second, she has a knack for finding problem dogs – the ones no one else can handle.

A small but significant backstory is that we met each other overseas. It was the first time I'd ever been traveling, and Mika was beautiful confidence. For years, she'd often

gone back to Poland, where she was born, and where she
lived until she was six.

We're in 1998 at this time.

She told me about her dog.

Tyja.

(Pronounced *Teeya*.)

A Rottweiler German Shepherd cross. Of all the combi-
nations! And Tyja's command of her surrounds, and her
abilities in the art of ferocity, let's say, were the stuff of
suburban legend.

When people went to Mika's parents' house in
Edensor Park and dared to enter the backyard, they first
had to survive *the Tyja test* – one hell of an examination.
Apparently, the dog would circle you. If she liked you she'd
give you a warning look, then nonchalantly wander away. If
she *didn't* like you, she'd growl and bare her teeth. A clear
and present directive. – Get your arse back inside.

After which, she'd follow you to the door, and once
behind it again, if you gambled on reaching out your hand,
she'd thunder into the security screen.

As for me?

What do you do when you meet a beautiful girl on your
first trip away and fall completely, maddeningly in love, and
you're coming back home before she is? You agree to take
some of her clothes home, risking drugs and hidden fire-
arms, and last days in Bangkok or Singapore.

Having passed the customs challenge with flying colors,
I arrived home and called her mum and dad, arranging
delivery, and, by default, to meet the legendary dog.

To be honest, I wasn't overly worried, even if I should
have been. I'd subscribed from a young age to the idea that
if you didn't show fear to a dog and took a commonsense

approach, you'd be okay ninety-nine percent of the time . . . although from everything I'd been told, Tyja was a one-percenter.

Like most car trips in Sydney, Mika's place was forty-five minutes to an hour away, and I was more than an hour early. I didn't park directly outside the house, but further down the cul-de-sac. When I walked up the driveway, I saw Tyja behind the gate, where she barked and showcased her teeth. This dog was here for business. I rang the doorbell nervously, for many more reasons than one.

When I went inside, Mika's mum and dad were very welcoming, a house with slate and light. We talked for a while, about traveling, and Mika, and I tentatively ate the fruit they'd brought out, till they asked the inevitable question.

Did I want to go out and meet Tyja?

Now, what was I going to say?

Look, I really love your daughter, but I don't have the guts to meet your ferocious dog?

I don't think so.

This was a time to prove myself. For both physical and mental fortitude.

When we opened the flyscreen, Tyja was further away, around the side of the house. For whatever reason, I was a stride or two ahead, and when Tyja saw me, she stopped. She studied me from a distance for scarcely more than a second, then she dug her ample paws into the ground and came careering in my direction. Big and black and muscular and gold, she launched herself through the air. She hit me – and started licking. She crowded against my legs the way only a dog can do, and she snuffed and pawed and continued. She licked my forearms and hands, those teeth both felt and suggested, but with excitement rather than terror. She lay down and flopped on her back. I crouched and rubbed her stomach.

To this day, Mika's mum, Halina, says she thought I was about to die. That sight, of Tyja midair, claws open. She'd never seen that dog react to anyone like that, but to be fair, I'm not deluded. I'm sure it was all in the scent. She could probably smell Mika from the laundry bag the moment I walked up the driveway.

Still, from that day onward, Tyja and I were tight – and as the story goes, when I left the house that afternoon, Halina rang Mika in Warsaw, and said, 'I just met your future husband.'

Both Halina and Tyja were right.

Up in that very future, the night Mika called across the hallway, Tyja had been gone for quite some time, but a similar dog was looming.

'Come and have a look,' she said, leaning in at the dog on screen. I told her I'd be there soon, that I was finishing reading through a chapter. It wasn't necessarily the plan, but later, when I came to bed, Mika was already asleep.

I was forced to look in the morning, though, when she shoved her laptop on the table. I was caught off guard in the kitchen, and there he was, in front of me.

This dog was something else.

He was brindle and dark and wild-looking. One of his earth-colored ears was flopped irresistibly forward. Four months old and pouting. Black lips and disarming eyes. You could see he was half hyena-like, but loaded with mottle and character. He had fifty-two grades of brown.

'Oh, shit,' I said.

'I know.'

I knew that usage well.

I know, and its accomplice – that smile. The sound of it, next to me, alive.

She peered closer at the image. 'Isn't he gorgeous?'

'Well, he's definitely *something*, but I'm not sure I'd call it gorgeous.'

'Oh, come on, he's *beautiful*!'

'Oh, yeah.' I couldn't help myself. 'Maybe in a just-got-out-of-jail sort of way.'

'Stop that!' She slapped my arm.

'Okay, *yes*,' I agreed, 'he's beautiful.'

For a roller coaster of seconds, I tried to find anything I could to make it all go away, and soon enough, I did: Reuben. The name above the photo said *Reuben*. My first three published books had a central character named *Ruben* in them. It was even in the title of the second one, *Fighting Ruben Wolfe* – spelled differently, but still a *Reuben*.

'Hey,' I said, 'I can't have a dog with that name. Remember *Fighting Ruben Wolfe*? I can't have a dog with the same name as a character in one of my books.' It was pretty solid reasoning, I thought. 'How egotistical is that?'

But Mika?

Many steps ahead, as usual. Try winning an argument with this woman. You can't.

'You're thinking about this all wrong!' I was sitting in kitchen quicksand. She was talking in exclamation marks, and warming to the task. 'Don't you see, it's a sign! You and this dog are *simpatico*.' Italics now as well. 'It's *meant to be . . .*' She zoomed in on the photo and we dived inside the animal, and all his deep-dark browns. 'Anyway, we can always change his name.'

Covering every angle – standard.

'Good thinking,' I said, 'that solves everything!'

Throughout the day, there were more conversations (the usual – whether now was really the time), but we looked at each other and knew. Mika had long decided, and I was complicit now, too. By the time the clock hit midnight, I was up again with *Bridge of Clay*, getting nowhere, and thinking about the dog. Mika was still up reading when I came to bed and capitulated. 'Okay, let's have one last look.'

It was like she was sitting on a spring.

She walked to her desk and came marching back, with the image of Reuben in her arms. We took that dreadful leap.

'*Come onnn*,' she said – quite cutely, I admit. 'How can we say no to that face?'

This time, as I examined the flopped-over ear, the wild in each eye, and the mutinous shades of brown, I deciphered a new message as well – totally fictitious on my part, naturally – of *Who would have me but you?*

Then call it what you will.

Fatigue. Recklessness.

I leaned back, half-laughed, and relented.

There was a great big sigh of no return, and I knew he was on his way. 'Okay,' slipped out of my mouth. Such a simple, perfect word, with so many ramifications. It wasn't that the last say belonged to me, but such choices need total agreement. This was over but only beginning.

Within another fifteen minutes, I was pulled down hard into sleep, and to dreams like twitching dog dreams. There were facts I knew to be immutable:

Reuben was out there somewhere, but he'd be here, with us, next day.

And next day came – and he was.

THE DOG WHO LOVED A GIRL

R euben was actually a very easy dog.
      To begin with.

True to his internet picture, he was a miniature, genial creature of multifaceted browns and charcoal – brown, black, darkest-brown, more-brown-but-lighter, then darker again – and a snout like he'd climbed from a coal mine. On his chest there was also a small diamond of white fur, but for the most part you never noticed it. His eyes said — I know I'm ridiculous, but I'll love you till there's nothing left of me.

His ears, wolfish triangles.

His paws were for growing into – he hoofed them to carry their weight.

Of course, there were early problems, like the typical puppy unruliness, and disfiguring some household items. Mika was pretty unimpressed with a gnarled pair of UGG boots, for example, but he wasn't overly destructive as far as four-month-old dogs go. She kept him in the house at night, too, and there were some fairly serious blowouts. She bought a new vacuum immediately – one with carpet-shampooing capabilities. (Such things don't work on cat urine, by the way – nothing does – but it was effective for the sins of the dog.)

I wasn't home that first day he arrived.

I have no memory of where I was.

What I remember is that my initial glimpse of him was at night, and he'd just been gored by Bijoux, who was staking his claim on the house. He was likely citing ownership of all the humans as well, and of course, the dog himself. That little tough guy was on him like white on rice. Crazy as it seems, I can't help but imagine the monologue. Each look was brimming with intent.

— Now listen, he broke things down for him. — How about we get this right from the get-go? It's me who calls the shots round here. Chase me and you die. Touch my food, you get *Jacksoned*. Look at me the wrong way, same again. In fact, don't come anywhere near me and there's a small chance I'll let you live.

The first time I ever saw Reuben in the flesh, he was loping down the hallway, crying.

I have to give it to Mika, though.

As the driving force behind the new acquisition, she knew the jury was still out where I was concerned, and she took on full responsibility. She walked Reuben, she fed him. She cleaned up after him. But more than anything, she just loved him. For weeks, she slept on the couch, on hand for the midnight toilet breaks, with the dog on the floor beside her.

Kitty, of course, adored him.

She was just on three-and-a-half years old, blond and still quite chubby-fisted, and Reuben came up to her waist. She sat and looked through books with him. They wandered around the backyard. A girl and her sweet little beast.

For me, as I've said, there was work to do.

Reuben would have to earn it.

I don't know why I took so much convincing – he was such an unusual animal. For the same reason I love an image that changes a sentence from exactly what you were expecting into something just left of center, Reuben was the perfect companion.

The first time I took him for a walk, we went to the local markets and a guy in a stall smiled broadly.

'What's that,' he asked, 'a hyena?'

I laughed and said, 'You bet.'

The world had definitely changed since I'd had a dog myself.

Actually, I'd never owned a dog at all, or I'd never been part of the decision. We had a Border Collie named Panda when I was growing up, and Panda lived almost exclusively out in the yard. He was around before I was born, and wasn't religiously walked. Compare that to now, where I can calculate an average of two dog walks a day over the last fourteen years or so. That's 10,000 dog walks, or more.

Sure, Panda had his moments, and a small share of family vacations. He was never overtly mistreated, but he was one of those poor unfortunate souls who was sworn of broken promises. My dad had vowed to walk, feed and clean up after him, but my mum was gifted the work – and with her own full-time job and the havoc of bringing up four children,

Panda didn't get much running. Or never as much as he should have. I mean, for Christ's sake, he was a Border Collie! It's funny the things we remember, though. Later in his life, I would always know when a storm was coming, because he'd slide the flyscreen door open with a paw or his snout, and quietly enter the house. I'd be sitting there doing homework with that feeling someone was watching me. Sure enough, I'd turn around, and there was the kind-eyed dog.

'Hey, Pand!' I would grin. 'Come on, come sit beside me.'

He made it to fifteen years.

That first outing together, Reuben and I doubled back from the markets to Centennial Park.

Another thing that had changed since my childhood was the need to carry dog-shit bags. (I won't go into it too much, but I refuse to call them *poo bags*; it's either *dog-shit bag* or *bog bag*. *Poo bag*'s just too polite.)

When it comes to those bags, it's simple. They're like the American Express ads – you don't leave home without 'em. I'll often find them in random jacket pockets, or in shorts taken out of the wardrobe. I might not have worn them in a year or so, but you can bet there's a bag there. Or I'll be out somewhere, wondering at the lump in my jeans pocket; it's a series of unused dog-shit bags. Honestly, you find them everywhere, and sometimes they go through the wash. They hold up surprisingly well.

As for Reuben and me, our first bag run was epic. We walked past the Waverley bus depot, intending to cross at York Road and make our way into the park. There's a giant iron gate on the left, into what we still call, to this day, *Reuben's Field*. We were outside the bus depot when Reuben let go on the footpath, and how do I put this mildly? At best, it was like someone just dropped their milkshake. At worst it was something monsoonal.

Oh my God, I thought, Jesus Christ!

I know, double blasphemy, but at the time it felt appropriate – that scene was downright biblical. Frantically, I started cleanup, an act of abject futility, and it's always moments like those when humans appear from nowhere.

To this day, I remember the bag count:

Seven.

Seven bags, and it was mostly ineffective.

Still, I did my best, and resigned at last to move on. Reuben just looked at me blankly, like he didn't understand the fuss, especially all my swearing, while he was climbing, mid-clean, through my legs.

And last, a rule to live by.

Do your best, but never look back.

Weeks turned into months.

The new year came and went.

Reuben grew, and there was all the usual guesswork about what particular breed he was. Breed and age, they're the obligatory questions, on streets and in dog parks everywhere. Even last week, I was out in the morning with the Frost, and a young woman asked what breed he was, how old, and if he was desexed *and* fully vaccinated. Only when I'd answered yes to the whole questionnaire did she allow her Vizsla pup to go near him.

Reuben had been advertised as a Great Dane crossed with a Labrador, but our suspicion is that *Labrador* just gets thrown in when no one really knows. That, and they want to soften things, to make the dog sound family friendly: 'Oh, *Lab*, that's okay then.'

For all we knew, Reuben was a mix of sixteen different breeds, and people had strong reactions to him; that dog knew how to polarize. For every person who said, 'Oh, he's beautiful,' another would say, 'Look, no offense, but that might be the ugliest dog I've ever seen.' Harsh, I know, but I didn't mind, because he was certainly an original. To this day, I've seen other big, brindle-colored dogs, but not one has looked quite like him. Often, they're brindle but short-haired, the kind of dog that's almost bare on the stomach. Reuben, however, had *fur*. It might not have been the pret-tiest fur, more like a personal bushland, but he carried it with a poise of his own. And call it however you see it – maybe Stockholm syndrome in a dog – but Reuben was finally growing on me.

By the autumn of 2010, we *were* becoming simpatico, just as Mika had predicted.

Then something we weren't expecting:

Each day he became more mine.

At times, I've worried as I'm writing all this that it sounds like I just took over. I wonder how it's happened this way, that it's me as the guy with his dogs. Often these things are simple. It's the person who always feeds them. In my case I think it's the earliness. I've always been the first one up in every house I've lived in, and when you're the only person awake, the dog is there, so you might as well walk him, and then you might as well give him his breakfast. Soon enough, they're ready for you every day. As Bruce, a friend of mine, once said: 'You know, I think they notice our breathing change, not long before we even wake up.' Maybe that's why I would often open my eyes, in the semi-light of 5 a.m., and see Reuben's beckoning head there.

Some nights he slept outside, in the sizable kennel we'd bought him, but he was mostly indoors on his bed. In the mornings we went to the park, or through streets and city laneways. When Mika, Kitty and I walked somewhere, he often came along, which could lead to errors of judgment.

On that note, I tied him up once, outside Eastgate – one of the busier hubs in Bondi Junction. A woman made a phone call to Mika from the number on Reuben's collar. He seemed pretty frightened, she'd said, and now I look back and speculate. It was far too much too soon, and maybe that's where I ruined him. That moment, exactly there.

For a long time, he was fine going back to busy shopping zones, but at a certain point in our future, he became increasingly anxious. He would bark and threaten customers, and when he sat he would always face a particular direction – his posture a perfect compass. True north for Reuben was home.

In the meantime, there were milestones.

A few fights, and rites of passage.

He was reaching big-dog stature, but was chased one day in the park by a posse of Malteses – the only dogs he was ever afraid of. He played with kids and visitors, or anyone who entered our yard. We had our share of disagreements, sure, and the usual catalogue of failures. (The refusal to come or stay, especially in public, is always a source of embarrassment, but with Reuben that period was short. We had rituals and he knew how to follow them.)

There became an agreed-upon routine.

Morning shift was me, and I took him every day to the valley in Centennial Park – a meeting place for dogs and their owners. Later, on afternoon or evening walks, we all took Reuben together.

Those mornings, he ran and jousted with a brigade of similar firebrands. There were Roo and Sam, whose owners were older – the man a figure like Lurch. Their children had all moved out, and the dogs were spoiled replacements. There was a couple with a dog called Soda (after Sodapop in *The Outsiders*), and we talked about those kinds of names in books and movies – like the guy called Steak and Fries in *City of God*, that incredible book and film from Brazil.

On weekends, there was a short-haired version of Reuben called Thyla (with a silent H) – named for the Thylacine, or Tasmanian Tiger. Pat and Clare, Thyla's owners, were the ones who first said, 'Should we meet in Reuben's Field?' The dogs ran and played simultaneously, or was it really their version of work? The rumble, the stages of impact. The face at so many angles. They were dogs with breath like thoroughbreds.

At the end of every session, I would whistle for Reuben to come – our language in three quick notes. He would find his place beside me.

By May, Mika was seven months pregnant.

Reuben was talkative and roguish. He'd grown big, he was tall and powerful, but more than that, he was fit. He had the big dark face of a German Shepherd and the chest of a decent middleweight. When he ran at you, it's what you looked at. He had the athlete's muscle-and-bone look, and he was still learning how to use it.

On walks and runs, he was great. He was never a rampant leash-puller, keen as he was to go out, and ready each dawn beside me. I woke and sensed the shape of him.

(And now I get that eye-burn, remembering all those mornings, how I'd turn and see him and whisper, 'Hey, Reub, you doin' okay?'

First words in the dark to a dog's head.

I'd go back to those mornings in a heartbeat.)

The best illustration of what defined Reuben, though, already so early on, was his undying love for the girl. From day one he was devoted to Kitty, and she was equally enraptured with him.

It's one of those long-held beliefs that most children want a pet at some point, but quickly lose all interest. That wasn't the case with her. To be fair, I think it's more common in general these days. Animals are part of the family. Dogs are in the house more, they sleep inside. They're in the living room, watching telly, a constant in daily life – and all of them have their talents, and Reuben's was being with Kitty. Every day was a tea party or picnic.

The only time Reuben wouldn't listen to me was when we were all in the park together. He would always stay with Kitty. Without fail, he would put himself between her and anyone near her. Not in a menacing way (at least not yet), but he was there as her sole protector. There was one evening, especially, where for whatever reason, I was in the park with Reuben, and Mika and Kitty met us later. When we left, we decided that I would walk Reuben home, and Mika and Kitty would drive. He was still off-leash at the time, and he stayed with me as long as he could. He resisted the urge to go after her, until finally he couldn't take it. He turned and sprinted off, calculating the risk. Obedience vs. rebellion. No matter how hard I called, I knew that dog was gone. He crossed the inner loop of traffic, intercepting them at the car. I was caught between my pride (I mean, that bastard, he disrespected me!) and his pure dedication to Kitty.

'Oh, Reuben!' she wheezed, the air whistling through her teeth, or lack of them. 'Reuby-boy, come here!'

He practically somersaulted into the car – bloody dog had turned into a gymnast. Then he sat in the back and they celebrated; Reuben with his full set of choppers, and the typical grin of the kid – those plinths of teeth and potholes.

'Hey,' Mika asked me, 'you coming?'

I looked at her with mock disgust. 'Looks like I don't have much choice!'

But last, and maybe my favorite item of proof, of Reuben's devotion to Kitty?

Most telling back then was this.

On the street, when she asked to walk him, we'd hand her the leash and call to him.

'Hey, Reub – Kitty's walking you now.'

He would stop, glance back and realize, and slow down his pace to match hers. He would calmly walk beside her, looking over now and then to make sure:

She was happy, she was safe. She was good.

It stayed like that till June.

In June he went for the plumber.

THE TURNING

As years go by as a dog owner, you hone and craft your answers to the most frequent comments and questions. In my time with Reuben and Archer, when someone said, 'Beautiful dogs,' I'd reply, 'Thanks, they've ruined my life.' If the person was taken aback, I would prove I was joking with a follow-up. 'In the best possible way, of course!' We'd laugh and continue walking.

When people asked what breeds Reuben and Archer were, I would often point to Archie, and say, 'Well, that one's probably a Lab Greyhound cross.' Then I'd wave at Reuben. 'And he's at least eight different dogs, I reckon – all of them cranky.' If I was in a particular mood, I'd form a composite answer. 'They're a special kind of breed,' I'd say, 'designed to destroy your life.'

But again, I'd be smiling, half-laughter.

Love's not always kind.

*

The more I think about Reuben now, all these years later, after his life and epic death, I'm sure he was many and varied percentages of six main possible prototypes:

Great Dane and Mastiff.

Wolfhound and German Shepherd.

Greyhound and possibly werewolf.

He made noises like Chewbacca.

I remember one afternoon in the Centennial Park valley. There was a mother and her young daughter – a little blond girl in school uniform. They couldn't get their German Pointer back. Reuben was doing what he always did, rousting with other dogs, but never straying too far.

He ran with the German Pointer, and as the mother and daughter kept calling her, growing more frustrated, I whistled for Reuben to come, and when the Pointer followed, I grabbed her. I returned her and they were incredibly grateful.

Next day, things were different.

The pair were in the park again, and Reuben and the Pointer were chasing each other. Reuben started up some noise – one of his more casual versions of Chewbacca. In terms of its menace-meter, it was probably around mid-range, somewhere between a calm conversation in Wookiee with Han Solo, and his strangling of Lando Calrissian.

'Hey, your dog's being vicious!' called the woman. 'You have to do something about him!'

You remember me, don't you? I wondered.

I called and Reuben came.

Then I apologized, quietly seething. This is what I get for helping you yesterday. 'I'm sorry he got a bit noisy,' I said, and we walked up into the forest. I guess it's hard to know the difference sometimes between a vicious dog and a vocal one, and I realize it never sounds good. When a dog gets all talkative near another dog's throat, it doesn't help when he looks like Reuben.

When we left, he sauntered beside me, like the wolf in *Little Red Riding Hood*. What tall and rugged ears he had. What a galactic, terrorizing growl!

He blended into the shade.

His teeth showed when he smiled.

One of the stranger notes about the valley in Centennial Park and its vast flat field at the bottom is that it's where Australia became the *Commonwealth of Australia* – that is, the nation it is now, in the eyes of the world. On January 1, 1901, the federation ceremony was held there. These days, there's a circular, Roman-looking monument, sort of like a mini-pantheon, right in the middle of the grass, and it suffers a grisly fate – habitually pissed on by dogs.

What does that say about our country, I wonder?

One part of me says, Jesus, is nothing sacred? But then, it's also farcically perfect, or maybe just appropriate, given our past. Great country, tortured history. A writer like Kurt Vonnegut would have known exactly what to say, like his treatment of 'The Star-Spangled Banner' in *Breakfast of Champions*. As for me, all I can say is that maybe nothing *is* sacred in Sydney, and certainly not to its dogs.

So, I guess, it goes.

Of course, one of those dogs with his own history in that valley was the beast I was growing to love.

A few small facts about Reuben:

1. German Shepherds didn't like him.
2. His very appearance in the park could start trouble.

As I've said before, he had a big black snout that reminded me of a German Shepherd's, and his face reminiscent as well, in its dark and sandy undertones. Sometimes I wondered if that was why they didn't like him. If ever there were Shepherds around, they immediately made him unwelcome. They knew he was of them, but not them. A counterfeit, a scoundrel. If there were two, they would downright pummel him.

Owners would call over, they'd apologize.

I'd wave and say it was all good, and it was, because Reuben could more than handle himself. There's also nothing in the internal dog manual that says they should always be nice. If things became overly heated and Reuben was copping a hiding, I was always ready to go in. Only once did I see him sit down, all fours, and face the opposite direction. — Enough, he was saying, I'm done.

As for the second point, about troublemaking, or what my dad prefers to call *shit-stirring*, sometimes we walked down into that valley and it looked like a Hallmark greeting card. Dogs were prancing and frolicking, playing nicely; their owners chatting cordially, nursing tea or takeaway coffee cups.

Then Reuben came – everything changed.

Somewhere between a dozen to twenty dogs would instantly be chasing him, barking and carrying on. Reuben's face was slung out sideways, eyeing the angry mob, as he sprinted frantically by me.

— They're coming for me, man, *oh shit!*

The pack would fall and tumble.

Reuben would climb to the top.

Then he'd set off running again, in an arc around the monument.

A woman remarked, quite drolly, once:

'Easy to see who the alpha dog is here,' and me, I didn't say anything. I thought, All he did was show up!

That said, about the worst thing that happened around then was a raging case of warts. Have you ever seen warts in the vicinity of a dog's mouth? It's pretty special, especially on a dog like Reuben. His big black jowls were like wet and slippery car tires. *Infestation* doesn't even begin. It was a rash, or hornet's nest of barnacles, on his lips, in his throat, on his tongue. Luckily, compared to human warts, they recede much more quickly, though it felt like a pretty long month.

As for the unhappy prospect of Reuben turning, the moment was edging toward us.

As winter started, everything was progressing well, with our dog by no means a saint, but he was big and brash and generous. He still hung around with Kitty, still walked at her pace on the street. He was gentle and kind with other children, too, yet sometimes, of course, overzealous. But nothing you'd think of as vicious. He was playful, he leapt and laughed.

Actually, maybe there was a kind of harbinger, because earlier that year, when Dana and Daniel and their daughters, Noa and Zoe, came to stay with us, the two girls (aged around eight and six at the time) returned to San Francisco with a new song. It went: '*Reu-ben, don't kill us! Reu-ben, don't kill us!*'

Which we all thought was pretty funny, until the turning came.

*

Sydney's not known for having bleak winters, but our house was always cold. It was beautiful during summer, but even in spring or autumn, it would be nice out on the street, and still winter inside that house. We decided to get some heating.

As the work was done, there was a handful of men, a heap of noise, and no apparent problems. One afternoon, we had to leave for some reason or other, and Reuben was left with the tradesmen. He was probably out in the yard, but the men were often in and out. Still no problems reported.

One cool, gray morning, the head plumber returned to finish some bits and pieces, and that was when it all disintegrated. He'd been with Reuben before, quoting the job and during the work, but this time he met a different dog.

I still see the poor guy, transfixed inside the doorway, as Reuben entered with presence. The look in his eye said everything; the gold inside was backlit. He was in some other place, his chest and legs steeped forward – ready.

Then, behold the bark.

It overflowed.

There was heat and fire, and his throat forewarned an outcome. Both Mika and I were dismayed, and before I could even say anything, Reuben lunged and rose and charged at him. He didn't quite rip the plumber's shirt buttons off, but it was frighteningly close, and a shock. If nothing else, he got his nose to him. I can't remember anymore if there was a salivary patch on the work shirt, but it's always how I imagine it. He wasn't hit by *teeth*, but they weren't far away – their strength of color, bone white. And their shape – the length and curvature.

Mika and I shouted in stereo.

'Reuben! Reuben, stop!'

He shrank back from the plumber, who was forgiving but also alarmed.

'Bloody hell,' I said, 'I'm so sorry, are you okay?'

'Oh yeah, he's just being protective . . . Looking after the place, and you guys.'

'But still – shit, I'm so sorry.'

He gathered his composure well. 'Forget it, it's all good.'

From Reuben, there was definitely an after-growl.

— Come one step closer, pal, see what happens.

Mika and I must have apologized a dozen times, maybe more.

We were hoping it was just an anomaly, a one-off.

It wasn't.

It was difficult to explain.

Reuben was desexed, as all our dogs have been.

He'd shown no signs of a vicious streak, but after that moment there were others. Before, when someone patted him on the street, whether asking my permission or not, Reuben obliged quite happily. Now there was a chance he might snarl, or worse, give them *the look*.

— How much do you like that hand, really? If you want, I can reduce it to a stump.

Also, he was always a dog who loved dogs.

Now he was prone to a brain snap or two. If he saw something he didn't like the look of, he would run straight over the top of it, then come trotting back, job done. It certainly wasn't the worst thing that could happen, more just something unruly, and I'd call an apology to the owner, but half the time they didn't even answer. They'd be looking down at their phone, lost in other worlds, and I'd put Reuben on the leash. I'd march him straight back home.

Mika and I would deliberate.

Was it us?

Were we *creating* a vicious animal?

She was due to give birth by then, which is a story all of its own, but also in terms of the dog.

What can I tell you about the arrival of Noah, our son?

He was born in early July on a glorious but windy morning.

Like Kitty, he came out quickly.

Reuben thought he was food.

Yes – you read that correctly.

In short, he wanted to eat him.

At just after five a.m., we drove to the hospital in the dark and Noah was born in the light. He was happy from the moment he came out. I know I'm making it sound easy, but there were the requisite realms of agony, all blood and flesh and adrenaline – the line between beauty and barbarism. Putting it mildly, Mika was heroic. Putting it bluntly, in the words of a nurse, who came in later that morning, 'Are you the one who got out of the bath and walked across the room with the head already out?'

Mika looked over to me, I nodded, and the nurse continued. 'Jesus, woman, you're made of steel.'

In a previous chapter, I might have said Kitty was a tough little hombre, but it was easy to see where it came from. As a man you feel pretty ridiculous. You get the lift back down to the car park. You sit speechless in the car. Only thoughts . . .

That was insane – incredible.

And, of course.

Thank God I don't have to do *that*.

In the few days Mika was in the hospital, we did everything you're advised to do as both the parents of a newborn and as dog owners. The number one theory is that you should bring back a used item of the baby's clothing and give it to the dog to smell. Apparently, it sends a message:

This one's coming home, so be friendly and give him some room. You *like* this smell, you'll love him!

Each time I came home from the hospital, I gave Reuben a good noseful of anything connected to Noah – a baby suit, a onesie, a shawl. He'd sniffed them more than happily.

I think he'll be okay, I thought.

The reality was, he was not.

To be honest, it wasn't quite ferocious, but not just a curious nudge, either. He didn't get too close, if memory serves me correctly. But I do remember that he growled at the foreign object, as if firstly he didn't like it, and second, it might be lunch.

What we came to understand in hindsight is that babies are obviously different. If nothing else, this book never implies that I'm an expert on dogs and their dog-thoughts – that's clear from the very first line – but what I've learned is that to some dogs, a baby doesn't smell like a human. It's something different altogether, which for some of them might include food.

Essentially, Mika sat on the couch, holding Noah. Reuben stepped closer – he was curious – then grumbled, then took a good lunge at the baby. A definitive move to attack. But

remember me saying that hell hath no fury like a man at
war with his dog? Well, compared to a mother's love and
protection, especially of a newborn, that hell is a triviality.
She folded Noah inside herself somehow, and struck a hand
straight out to the dog.

'No! *Reuben – NO!*'

He stopped, stepped back, and sat. Then he hung his
head and wandered away, before returning to lie at Mika's
feet. He never did it again. As we've seen, and to be fair
to him, Reuben was a capable student, but I still wouldn't
blame you for thinking we were completely out of our
minds. There were plenty of people who told us: '*That* was
when you should have got rid of him – he lunged at your
newborn child!'

And maybe we really should have.

Apart from the worry of our children and their safety, it
would have spared us so many other ordeals, of mishap and
staggering vet bills. But hear me when I tell you – Reuben
was one of ours. We couldn't just abandon him.

(And again, I hear the voices:

'Of course you could, you had to! What are you, bloody
insane?!')

But no, we would never quit on him.

We believed in his ability to learn.

We believed in him as Kitty's greatest friend in the
world. What would we have said to her? 'Sorry, kid, say
goodbye to your dog.'

Well – no.

We had to keep him. We took him on and we promised
to love him, and that was what we intended to do. Mika, as
someone who considers the love and purity in animals as far
superior to that of humans, didn't even mention getting rid

of him. Mother's love was one thing, but loving animals, too, was worth it.

In both the background and forefront of our thinking, of course, was the memory of tragic news stories, of family dogs who've seriously hurt someone, or worse. (Let's face it, people have died.) But there's always that belief, *It's not us.* That thought, *We won't allow it.*

So that's when you make the vow.

We watched him perennially. Meticulously. There was never a time of nonvigilance – and we witnessed what we'd hoped for. We saw Reuben love Noah exactly as he'd always loved Kitty, with honor and unending duty.

And Mika and me?

Okay, I admit it, there's a chance we were probably delusional. Who would keep this dog but us? Surely, no one else was up to the task. He was faithful to us, we'd be loyal to him. It would all be okay – we deserved it.

But how many universal truths, and their corresponding counterpoints, can hit you like that all at once? The surest way to *not* get something is to feel like you're somehow owed it:

You take in a dog.

The dog's problematic.

You do a good deed and you keep him. You don't ditch him at the first signs of trouble . . . Oh yes, you've done the right thing, all right. Good karma will always come back.

And no good deed goes unpunished.

THE DOG WHO KNOCKED
ME OUT

There's no nonhumiliating way to put this:

In January of 2011, Reuben knocked me out in the park.

He busted my knee. I was knocked out cold.

That's what I call good karma.

Even to this day, all these years later, I love Reuben and miss the hell out of him – but honestly, what a *prick*.

One of the nicer things about writing books, between the doubts, the fears and noncompletions, is that you learn what your obsessions are, both the obvious and the hidden. There are certain threads that appear in almost everything I've written.

Running and training.

Colors and sky.

Stories within stories.

And animals – and by animals, I mostly mean dogs.

Look at my first three book titles: *The Underdog, Fighting Ruben Wolfe, When Dogs Cry*. Across almost everything I've published, there have been dogs, both central or as cameos. I've had a coffee-drinking dog called The Doorman in *I Am the Messenger*. (One of my favorite characters I've written, the fact that I was poisoning him with caffeine notwithstanding.) There was the Pomeranian heart attack victim named Miffy in the Wolfe trilogy. Then Rosy the Border Collie, who rounds up the clothesline in *Bridge of Clay*. Perfectly enough, it's only *The Book Thief* that doesn't have a dog – just the brief appearance of a bent-whiskered cat, modeled on Brutus. That aside, dogs have been an essential part of my writing personality. I've rendered them with care and devotion, I've written them with love and joy, which brings us to the necessary question.

What does that owe me in life?

The answer, of course, is nothing.

Previous to having my own dogs, I'd always conjured up images of optimism – of dogs who lived only for loyalty. Dogs who followed me everywhere. Dogs who were great and golden. And I've received that, I really have, but it's not the entire picture.

As it stands now, the gifts have been far greater, because perfect dogs, identical to perfect lives, are pretty dull. Do you want your dog to be uncultured, unkempt, uncivilized? Of course not. Do you want him to roll in human waste in those haunted bushes in the park? No way on this planet, believe me – I've scrubbed those necks and collars.

And of course, the moment I've been leading to:

Do we want our nearly forty-kilo, fit, formidable mongrel of a dog to come crashing into us from the side, while we're holding our six-month-old child?

Answering that one is pointless.

The morning it happened was cloudy.

When accidents happen, I have a tendency, probably like most people, to wonder if things might have gone differently if I hadn't made one small decision. On that morning, just before six o'clock, I made two.

First, I had coffee before I took Reuben out, whereas normally I'd wait till we returned. Second, whenever I took Noah with me, which was rare, I carried him on my right arm, walking Reuben on-leash with the left. Then I'd let him off in the park. (We never had problems bringing Noah along, and carrying him was easier than pushing the stroller, dealing with the grass, the tree roots, the rocks.) This time, though, I'd finally figured out how to work the BabyBjörn carrier, and Noah was strapped to my chest. Maybe if I hadn't made either of those decisions, I'd have made it through that morning conscious.

Around quarter past six, we walked down to the valley of dogs, maybe fifty meters from the monument. There was a handful of people and their charges. I was talking to a woman named Valerie, who was also talking to Noah. Usually, I kept a good eye on Reuben, but that morning I was distracted.

Imagine being hit by an iron bar, or a woodchopper's axe, at the knee.

That was how Reuben got me.

He and Valerie's dog – a Ridgeback with the innocent

name of Bertie – had come galloping in our direction. Reuben's head was more lethal than kryptonite; I went down, hit the ground, knocked out.

On the way, I said, 'Is he okay?'

I was trying to get a look at Noah.

When I woke up, he was bouncing happily in the arms of a young woman named Molly – and Reuben, showing all his love and gratitude, was still tearing around with Bertie.

As if the morning hadn't been mortifying enough, while I was regaining my senses, an ambulance was called. There were park rangers, more people, dogs in all directions, and Noah laughing his head off. When I climbed back to my feet, it was difficult to stand or walk, and things were about to get worse.

Mika was called by someone at the scene.

She was still in bed with Kitty.

When they came down, it was Mika who convinced me to *just get in the goddamn ambulance, okay*, and I did and felt like an idiot. By then I was sure I could walk.

Before I left, we got Molly's number, and a few days later, we sent her a gift. (It was a notebook with Shaun Tan illustrations, I can still see it. When it comes to humiliating history, our memories are at their sharpest.) In the ambulance I made a decision, in the foglands of shame and embarrassment, but one I could never quite keep.

Our days in Centennial were over.

I could never go down there again.

But what is it about moments like those, and dogs we own like Reuben? Depending on how we look at them, they're gifts that just keep giving.

Just as life not going to plan will give us the best of our stories, the *nobbling* incident was a favor, and with Reuben it was just the beginning. Within the next year, he would have the first of two knee reconstructions, at five thousand dollars a pop. Then, to bookend the whole experience, nearly a decade later, in June 2020, after Reuben was no longer with us, I finally needed knee surgery myself, from that fateful morning in the park. It was definitely very Reuben. He even got me from the grave, and I'm grateful. I'm also glad it was me he injured, and not Noah, or someone else. That could have been catastrophic. To be honest, I even loved him later that same morning, when I'd returned from my trip in the ambulance and the very brief check in the hospital. He was back inside the house, and walked past me in the kitchen, stepping right into the flesh of my toes. The reflex ignited my knee, and I nearly hit the ceiling.

'WHAT'S THAT FUCKING DOG DOING IN HERE?!'

But by then it was pretty obvious.

I knew exactly why Reuben was in the house, and in the kitchen, and in my life:

That dog was born for stories.

For love and projects of mayhem.

And more in the world to come.

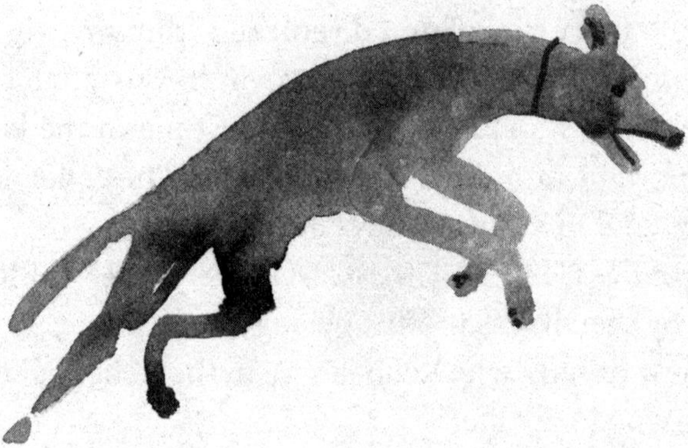

part two

REUBEN &

ARCHER

THE DOG MY DAD CALLED
LUCIFER

After the knockout in the park, life went on, it always does, but with a bruised and dislocated pride. Sometimes it's hard to pop all that back in, and you wonder if you'll ever leave the house again. At other times, I feel like much of my experience is relearning that humiliation is only personal. No one else really cares.

You got knocked out in public by your dog?

Jesus, that's hilarious!

You got a terrible review for your latest book?

Bummer, man, pass the salt.

We dwell on these moments alone, and the world moves on without us till we're coaxed or dragged back in. Or some – the bravest among us – seem to find the nearest diving board and plunge straight back into the whirlpool.

The knockout in the park was significant in other ways, too, especially looking back now. It feels like a dividing line, as the first real instance of truer, more heightened chaos.

Previous bad behaviors were one thing, but this was a struc-tured *unstructured* dysfunction. It was anarchy almost by design. Ambulances. Hospital. Fallen babies. Concussion victims. Rangers. Public attention. Bertie the bloody Ridgeback!

It's also a sort of stepping stone, edging us nearer to the appearance of Archer.

Over the next few months, there was some physio on my knee, which worked, but not completely, and Reuben and I became friends again. Actually, that part happened sooner. I couldn't be mad at him for more than a day. We even went back to Centennial, eventually. (There are plenty of other options where we live, especially the steeper, more rain-foresty Cooper Park, where I go most days with Frosty.) Either way, I couldn't walk too well for weeks, and Mika took Reuben out instead. As someone more civilized than me, she waited till later in the morning, but soon enough I reached my limit. I ignored the small tear in my knee, and it healed, but never quite properly.

What I often forget are the good times – the great times! After his initial skepticism of Noah, it bears confirming that Reuben loved him unconditionally. He also continued his love and protection of Kitty, who remained a constant playmate. In that regard, he was so gentle it was astounding. He snuffled treats from out of her fingers. You'd have thought he had no teeth.

I loved walking him every dawn again, and later in the afternoon. Sure, I was half-limping, but even that faded to just that small glow of pain we can live with. One of the more useful parts of dog ownership is that they get you out of bed every day, even when you don't really feel like it. If you're sick, they get you moving. If you're down, they get you up. They're the best personal trainers in the world.

There are moments I view like a slide show now – you might know the ones I mean – where the lights go out in someone's living room, and you watch their childhoods, or their vacations from the '60s, '70s or '80s. There's the click and that circular movement. Next image on the wall, or a bedsheet.

I watch Reuben dismantle a football, lace by lace, then hack his way through the leather. He chews sticks till they're pulverized to breadcrumbs. He picks up giant palm fronds a few meters long and tows them across the ground. It was all in a good day's work.

Then a firm and family favorite – he's lying on his bed having *running dreams*, steering legs and tangled paws. He whimpers across his sleep. Even motionless, he was worth looking at. His legs would often remind me of things, but mostly of firewood or kindling. He was a dog of bark and branches.

But again, the pendulum swings, because the good came with certain baggage, like random acts of violence; a quick trampling of a Cocker Spaniel, or a lunge at a Miniature Poodle. Though none of them were ever hurt, I would always come down hard on him. Fierce words and tight on the leash. It was then he'd go all Eeyore on me, but I never made room for pity. With dogs like Reuben you have to mean it.

There was a Sunday morning when some friends, James and Mardi, came over – two writers and their young daughters. They were the kind of friends we knew but didn't know well. Our children were similar ages.

What I remember is that nobody went into the back-yard on account of the cold and drizzle. Reuben was outside on the covered back porch, and every time the couple's two-year-old daughter moved closer to the door, you thought he might come through the glass.

I think James and Mardi were horrified. They haven't been to our house ever since. Not so much a *vicious dog* thing, I hope. More just that sometimes that's how life goes, but Reuben didn't help, put it that way.

My favorite story of that period was when my dad came over to stay, in late July. My dad's a retired housepainter, and he was touching up some window frames we'd just had repaired, and for me there are two strong memories.

One was when he saw me reading on the couch to Noah, who was now just over a year old. He said, 'You're a better father than I ever was – I never read to you at all.'

'And look what happened,' I said, 'I became a writer.'

What I neglected to remind him was that books were everywhere in our house when my siblings and I were growing up. I also marveled at my dad hearing something on the news, then looking it up in his beloved *Encyclopedia Britannica*. 'Where *is* that place?' or 'When did that bloody war start again?' he'd be muttering to himself, wandering to the bookshelf in his overalls. The thing that really made me a writer was believing the lies of fiction – being capti-vated by novels and *living them*. I often say I love movies because I get to see the characters; I love books because I *become* the characters. What helped, growing up, was knowing that someone cared enough to have books in the bedrooms, the kitchen, the living room, even if they were just lying around. Even my dad's *Reader's Digest*, which he read in the bathroom, was a signal that stories mattered.

Yes, I know I should have told him all that, and so much more – not least because the one lesson I consistently learn as a parent is that you can't make your children love what you love, or what you *think* they should love. I should have told my dad he did it perfectly – just leave a few clues in the hope that your kids will pick one up. I was the luckiest among my siblings because what I picked up was the books. But all of it's relative, of course.

The second memory was dog-related.

How could it not be?

It was my poor old dad, seventy-eight at the time (he's nearly ninety-one now), getting up in the night for the bathroom. In the morning, he said, 'Did you hear that last night? When I got up to take a leak?'

We were sitting at the kitchen table, my dad in his paint-flecked overalls and a flannelette shirt, silver-haired and mischievous, as ever. He was smiling over his coffee.

'Last night?' I asked. 'What happened?'

He might not have read to me as a child, but my dad's a natural born storyteller. He knew how to build the drama.

'Well, as you know' – cue the decrepit, disintegrating voice – '*I'm only an old man* . . . So you know I have to get up two or three times every night for a piss.' Laughing now, great amusement. 'Only I get into the hallway and I see this dark shadowy figure at the other end, like a gargoyle – and it's growling – and it's got these two bright yellow eyes, just *glaring* at me . . .' His voice intensified, but getting quieter, the last two words a whisper. 'Just glaring at me – *like Lucifer.*'

'Shit,' I said, 'you should have called me straight away.'

'I couldn't, I was paralyzed!'

'So what did you do?'

Again, that rascally smile. 'I took one step, and so did he. I said, "Reuben, it's me, it's *Helmut*," and he turned and walked away.'

'Was he there when you came back out?'

'No, and believe me, I *checked*. He must have gone back to sleep. But let me tell you, two hours later, when I had to go again, I decided to wait till morning.'

'Jesus, Dad, I'm so sorry!'

'Oh nah,' he said, 'it was funny – well, sort of, even if I feared for my life . . .' Then he leaned toward me gravely again, coffee in hand. 'From now on, though, I'm calling him Lucifer.'

'That's okay, Dad, fair enough.'

And true to his word, he did.

'Hey, Lucifer!' my dad would call from that point on, every time he came over, and Reuben would lie on his back. He'd get a good stomach-rub, and his jowls would curtain to the floor. Their midnight meeting was forgotten.

Now as I sit here and write about it, that scene from the night dissolves. Those hellfire eyes in the dark, and the intent of impending assault. It's the last story I think of when there was us and only Reuben – for at the end of that darkened hallway, when the eyes die down and my dad returns to bed, out of the black climbs someone else.

Bright fur, a broken object.

Looking closer, I see a street dog.

The golden, glorious Archer.

It's funny the things we remember, too, because not long after we got him, I did a talk for a writing workshop in Crows Nest. The teacher of the class was James, whose visit to our house was now legendary, for the dog attacking the glass. Later, when I told him we'd taken on a street dog as well, he couldn't hide his amazement. He was still envisaging Reuben doing his best Tyja impression, launching at the door with fury.

'You did *what*?' he said. '*Another* one?!'

In so many ways he was right.

A STREET DOG AND A
MOVIE STAR

Something happened in 2011.
 But first.
Let me just say.
Archer.
Blond, beautiful, long-legged, street-scarred, handsome, wild, gentlemanly Archer.
What a combination, and contradiction.
Gone at the time of writing.
I miss him every day.

Right from the start, it was meant to be, and he was, as I've said, quite handsome. Even now I think of movie stars – a parade of blonds, and blondes:
 Brigitte Bardot, Brad Pitt, Jane Fonda. Daryl Hannah. Heath Ledger. Paul Newman, Kiefer Sutherland (oh man, that hair in *The Lost Boys*). Grace Kelly! The list is never-ending.

In the beginning he was terribly skinny.

He had beauty and killer instinct.

And he achieved what I thought unthinkable – he put an end to my superstitions.

You'll see what I mean pretty soon.

What happened that year was the death of a dog.

Mika's mum and dad – Halina and Jacek – had Rocky and Scooby at the time, and the chivalrous Rocky died. He was a cross between a Boxer and a Staffy, and he was one of the sweetest dogs we'd ever known.

Mika and I bought him from an outer-suburban shelter in 2000, as a present for Halina, and as company for Tyja. When Tyja died in 2006, Rocky ran away to find her, crossing several lanes of traffic. While Mika walked the streets with Kitty in the stroller, I remember driving through Sylvania and Gymea (where Halina and Jacek lived at the time) with that sinking feeling in my stomach. Would I glimpse him dead on the road somewhere? Luckily, I didn't.

Hours later, on the other side of the busiest nearby street, The Boulevarde, Halina and I were out looking on foot. It was getting close to dark. When I came across a couple out walking, I asked, 'Have you seen a dog by any chance, black and white? A bit lanky?'

'What – like that one?' they said.

Sure enough, there he was.

He was the sort of dog who looked a bit unsure even when he was happy, but he was ecstatic as he loped toward me. I was so relieved, and I've never seen anything like my mother-in-law as she came running toward us to hug him. It was the closest I've ever felt to being in a movie, where the lovers run to each other and embrace. Comedy aside, it was just that; just love. Best thing that night in the suburbs.

By 2011, Rocky was breaking down, his squarish head caving inward. He had cancer of some variety, and soon the time came. Scooby – the big black Lab Great Dane cross, was on his own.

This time Halina decided not to search for a permanent replacement (it becomes an endless cycle), but to start fostering dogs instead, before a suitable owner is found for them.

When I heard this news, I was doubtful.

'You know what's going to happen,' I said to Mika. 'She'll fall in love with the first dog she fosters and keep it.'

Boy did I read *that* one wrong.

I'm sure you know what happened.

It was me who would take that dog in. There's a sucker born every minute.

When Halina joined the foster program, the first dog was a bit of an unknown. All Mika and I knew was that he'd been a street dog. I was expecting something mangy and withered, or maybe out of a cartoon – like the oversized bulldog who beats up Sylvester all the time in *Bugs Bunny* for trying to gobble up Tweety Bird. What greeted me was a shock.

He had fur like golden sand.

Long, *long* legs.

Longing, honey-colored eyes.

When they brought him over, Jacek was in the house first. He probably brought Scooby in while Halina took care of Archer. Apparently, the dog was a cross between a Staffy and a Labrador, and when I asked Jacek what his name was, he said something I'll never forget.

A few things about my father-in-law – he was the kindest, most softly spoken man you could ever hope to meet, and talked with a strong Polish accent. He was patient and extremely knowledgeable, and had a knack for tech and woodwork. What he didn't have a knack for was names.

(We lost him in October 2022, and I can't tell you what it's done to me in my edits here, to change tense from present to past. It doesn't take much to see him here, though – an archangel of grudging dog ownership. See, his dogs were always Halina's dogs, but he loved them just as much, I think, especially while denying it. He'd be smiling, going, 'Hard life with these dogs, Markus, and terrible life with this lady, my wife . . .' Smiling because he knew it to be the opposite.)

When I asked him the dog's name, he spoke in his typically bewildered manner: 'Honestly, Markus, I have no clue.' Then he stopped and had a good think. 'Maybe something starting with A.'

The dilemma would be all in the details.

From Mika's dad to mine, my own is very superstitious, in a multitude of ways. A few examples? The Zusaks have a lucky number; it's thirteen. If you break your leg, my dad will say, 'There was a reason for that – you never know what it's good for!' Which will lead you to ask something ludicrous.

'You mean if I hadn't broken my leg, I might have gone out tomorrow and broken my neck?'

'Exactly!'

He has rituals of far-flung meaning, like what day to wash your socks, or which direction to stir a paint pot, and for how long.

My favorite superstition of my dad's is the one on New Year's Eve where he takes down every towel in the house, as well as anything else hung up to dry. T-shirts, swimwear, *everything*, and why? So that you're not starting the new year with unfinished business from the last one. You can take care of that on January 2. (I know, it defies belief.)

But, and it's a big one, he'd passed the same witchcraft on to me. Even in childhood I was always superstitious, especially when it came to sport. I never changed my underwear the morning of a football game, for instance; although, to be honest, there's a practicality in that as well, because it'll only get dirtier in the game. Additionally, I would only tape up my boots with black electrical tape. Any other color was bad luck. Once, I was out of black and used gray, and suffered the drastic consequence – I kicked out twice on the full and missed a conversion from next to the posts. The game was a semifinal. When I missed that easy shot at goal, I heard someone shout from the crowd: 'YOU'RE A SHOCKER, NUMBER SEVEN!' Good training for dealing with critics.

In terms of my other superstitions, there were many.

As a teenager, I collected stones for luck, and kept them in my left pocket – never the right; the right pocket was where my wallet would go, and I didn't want luck touching money.

When I wanted to become a writer, I would always give myself start times. If I was supposed to start at 7 a.m., and it hit 7:01 and I still hadn't begun, I'd go, 'Well, that's *that* day shot then.' (Probably procrastination as much as superstition.)

I would also get out of bed at night, dozens of times before sleeping, to make notes for any and all future book ideas. I'd lie awake, telling myself, 'Don't think, don't think,' but even that was thinking *something*, so I'd get up again and write it in my notebook. Doing the work, even on grounds of purely irrational motivation, would get me where I needed to go.

In theory, I did always realize the medieval silliness of it, but there was part of me that couldn't let it go. I liked the idea of routine, I liked my little rituals. I put faith in the concept of karma, despite knowing its flaws and fallacy. I persisted with certain performances and believed in earning your luck.

As a parallel, I believed in fate, too, in the world and its wild deliverance. Sometimes we're sent good luck charms – we just have to read the signals. And yes, I believed in heeding them.

Until that dog, the blond one.

By September 2011, I'd written hundreds of beginnings to *Bridge of Clay*. There were countless edits of prologues. A sludge of half-cooked chapters, most of them gone cold. I had thousands of written pages, and maybe a hundred or so I could live with.

But I still felt so far away.

An end was inconceivable.

I would return, time and again, to the *first* page, as if starting over was the answer . . . and another thing I can promise you – the answer *wasn't* getting a second dog. But that's exactly where it all converged. Books, failures, superstition. Decision.

In *Bridge of Clay*, Clay Dunbar and his family live in Sydney, and from day one, their address was 18 Archer Street. I was six hard years into writing it when the dog walked down our path. Jacek's *A*, of course, was for *Archer*.

When I heard it, I couldn't help myself.

'You've gotta be kidding me!'

Everyone looked over, but Halina did the talking. 'What?' she asked. 'What is it?'

'My book,' I said, 'my characters – they live on a road called Archer Street.'

Our kitchen fell eerily quiet. We all knew my superstitious nature, and in a matter of seconds we were all swept inward to one of the more ominous warning calls of them all – the whisper unspoken, but heard.

This dog, was surely, good luck.

Something that interests me is that we could have changed Reuben's name back in 2009, but despite my reservations about both his name and the dog himself, it never occurred to us in the end not to keep it. Reuben was Reuben. It fit.

Then exactly the same with Archer.

And now Frosty. (Despite Mika's pleas for Ziggy.)

For whatever reason, I like that fact. Maybe it's the idea that we took these animals as they were. If the name was good enough for the group home, it was good enough for us. The way I see it, there needs to be a pretty good reason to change those names, as was the case with Rocky – his original name was Stalin. Not so great for most people, but especially Polish immigrants.

Halina is an animal lover, but has a special affinity for dogs, so the fostering idea was a good one. She just couldn't quite go through with it. Sure, my prediction that she'd keep the first dog she fostered might have missed the mark, but Halina and Jacek kept the second one, Atlas – a book in himself, just not this one.

As far as taking Archer went, the problem with a superstitious nature is the thought that if you resist, or worse, *reject* the good fortune staring you in the face, you might be invoking *bad* luck. Totally preposterous, naturally.

To compound the situation, we heard the sad tale of the dog. He'd survived parvovirus, which was something we'd never heard of. It attacks the gastrointestinal system and it's a hard one to come back from, especially if you're unwanted, unloved. Archer, it would seem, was both. From what Halina knew, he'd been found on the street. He didn't have fur on his stomach, and patches were missing elsewhere. Yet he was somehow still quite beautiful, like Marilyn Monroe on a downer.

Of course, Mika and I considered it.

Again, we talked positives and negatives, most often at the kitchen table, and this time it was me who was more in favor. Breed-wise, the greater likelihood was that he was a Lab Greyhound cross, and he was handsome, and seemed to be placid. (Note, *seemed*.) We covered everything from Kitty, Noah, cats, Reuben (not to mention Reuben on the spectrum of vicious), and realized it was all a handful. Every now and then, though, I was susceptible to saying, 'But Archer Street, for God's sake. This dog – he might be good luck.'

To which Mika gave me the look. 'He can't write the book for you, you know that, don't you?'

I laughed. 'If only he could.'

It took about a fortnight, but at some point, we knew. Archer was going to be ours. Mika even told me recently that it was Jacek who finally convinced her, guilting her over the phone with his notoriously quiet sledgehammers. Things like, 'Markus really wants him, I think, and isn't he always good to you? Doesn't he give you everything *you* want?'

So, for the second time in as many years, we took the dreadful leap. On a Sunday afternoon, I spoke to the head of the foster care organization and was deemed an acceptable owner. (If only they knew my incompetence!) I was out in the yard with Kitty, Noah and Reuben, and I remember us walking back inside.

'Well,' I said, 'looks like it's done.'

Mika smiled, she couldn't help it. 'Archer?'

I nodded.

'Okay then,' she said, 'let's see if he really *is* good luck.'

She didn't sound too convinced, and to be honest, neither was I.

The following week I was in America, giving workshops in Tampa, Philadelphia, and a university up in Kutztown, Pennsylvania. (I remember the drive from Philadelphia really well. The driver was a mad conspiracy theorist and made myriad memorable tirades. My favorite was, 'If they

ever take my guns away, I'm moving down to Australia!'
I had to tell him he might be disappointed, given I don't
know a single person who owns a gun.)

When I arrived home, I was expecting to pick Archer
up in the next few days, but when I walked down our
path, I heard a pair of dogs in freefall. They were clearly
in the middle of some sort of deep and meaningful power
struggle – shouting, arm-wrestling, bitching, moaning,
arguing, scrapping, leg-biting, ear-nipping, neck-savaging
and so on.

'Is that,' I asked Mika, 'what I think it is?'

And honestly, I have to give it to her.

She laughs in these situations – mostly.

'Yes,' she said, 'it is.'

Reuben's head peered around the wall, the embodiment
of incredulity.

— About bloody time you got home! Are you hearing this
shit?

When I made it through the house and out the back, the
dogs were rolling around, fighting for control of Reuben's
bed. Archer, at six months old, was giving as good as he got.
He especially had a knack (a portal to times ahead) for going
in hard for the throat.

The barking increased.

More wrestle.

It was a dog's breakfast of jaws and legs – and Mika,
patting me on the shoulder.

'Welcome home,' she said, and escaped back inside.

I called out beseechingly, behind her:

'He's good luck! Good luck, I tellya!'

The voice, now further in. 'Oh yeah, I can already tell!'

Both dogs were breathing heavily. Blondly, brownly.
Steadily, they eyed me, waiting.
'What?' I asked.
More breathing.
The storms of fate were brewing.

SONS & BROTHERS

Despite everything that happened when Reuben and Archer combined forces over the years, I loved Archer as much as any man loved any dog, and I wouldn't give him up for anything. (And naturally, same for Reuben.)

A random memory hits me:

In later years, Archer followed me everywhere. Whenever I walked up our stairs, it was like a slapstick comedy. Archer would walk beside me, always on the left, against the wall, quiet, sheepish and handsome. When I stopped, he stopped. He'd give me a guilty look. When I took a step, he took a step. Another step, *he* took another step, and still with the guilty expression. It was endlessly entertaining.

Mika would say, 'Looks like your old faithful's going up with you again,' and I'd smile, I felt such warmth for him. I'd place a hand down onto his head. 'You comin' up, Archo?'

(He was Archer, Archie, Arch, Archerbald, Baldo, Baldilocks, and also, as mentioned, Archo, which led to

Archo-Groucho-Zeppo, and too many more to go on with. In the end, he was also just Buddy, or Bud. '. . . Come on, Bud, let's go up.' He lay in my office on his bed, he looked so great in the sun – and yes, I'm all teary as I write this.)

Damn memories, damn dogs, damn *all of it*.

They break your heart.

For such a gentle dog in the end, he was hard to work with initially. I guess it's a simple truth that with foster dogs, rescue dogs, pound dogs, even purebreds, you never really know what you'll get. Add *street dog* into the mix and it's code for *they don't mind a scrap* – both the food variety and the niggle. Archer never backed down from a fight, *or* a chucked-out, disgusting bit of Kentucky Fried. I had to watch him when we walked the streets. One chowed-down chicken bone could kill him.

As for the fighting, there's debate to this day as to who was really in charge between him and Reuben; often it was hard to tell. They were also, for all intents and purposes, twice separated, due to Reuben's future knee reconstructions, and the subsequent long recoveries. That didn't help much either.

Me, I still think it was Reuben.

To me he was like the king, or head honcho. As years went by, if someone came to the house, he'd take a quick glance and hang back, and Archer would do the dirty work. It was like Reuben had sidled up to him and said — Right, get your arse down there and *intimidate*. Crack a few heads if you have to, or don't come back at all.

On the other hand, maybe Archer just held Reuben in such awe that he was religiously trying to impress him.

In the park, though, or on the beach, if we threw a stick, Reuben would always win it, then Archer would get it off him, every time. But now I'm getting ahead of myself.

The first outings together were fine, but I was making the mistake of walking them one either side of me, where later I kept both of them on my left – using myself as a buffer between them, pedestrians and other dogs.

For the first few months, Archer wouldn't let anyone pat him on the head. He didn't bite or bark, he'd only shrink away, so at home, or waiting at traffic lights, I crouched and patted his chest. He was slowly accumulating fur there. When finally he allowed his head to be stroked, it was only us, immediate family. For the rest of his life, he didn't let people touch him there, with very few exceptions. (Also, regarding his coat, once restored it was sleek and healthy, but his shedding was fairly momentous – a dog who doubled our cleaning.)

Off-leash, he was predominantly okay, but when he misbehaved he did it in style. He was highly, frustratingly *strangleable*. There were the usual problems of recall early on, when he was running with other dogs – the art of calling your dog back and knowing he'll actually come – but they were nothing compared to when it was just him, Reuben and me. There were times he just blatantly refused, and if I said a single hard word he'd be so afraid that he'd approach in concentric circles, starting at fifty meters.

Jesus, I'd be thinking, we're going to be here all day.

Reuben would be sitting beside me, perfectly straight and still.

— Really? You think this dope's good luck?

If he were human he'd have turned and spat, or shaken his head in disgust.

As it happened, the first major problem we had wasn't so much with Archer, but Reuben. Before, he'd loved other dogs (okay, yes, there was the odd running-over-a-spaniel trick), but now whenever another dog was on the scene, Reuben was hackling up. In Archer he had a rival, and they would compete for the other dog's attention. They both had to get there first. I waited for a moment like this one:

They'd see another dog.

They'd turn on each other and fight.

Then, at some point, they'd shrug and come to an agreement. — Since we're beating up each other, we might as well beat *him* up too.

But they couldn't, not really. I was always close by, so there were incidents, yes, but no injuries. In all those years, I never had to pay another dog's vet bill (isn't that a baseline for things to be proud of?) but let's just say it was close. They were increasingly more than a handful.

On the street was tame in comparison to our place, though.

I remember their first big fight.

Before I get to it, however, I want to be fair. It wasn't *always* like this. There weren't fifteen outbreaks of violence every day; most often they were really bonding. They ran together, or tussled. Even if sometimes it sounded ugly, they were dogs just being dogs. Wild animals learning domestics. I hope you know what I mean.

Later, when I swapped one dog over to have them both

on my left-hand side, their ribs touched, their fur blended, they walked together in unison. They could honestly look like soldiers, especially as Archie grew even taller, and they were essentially the same height. Sometimes, when we walked down Queen Street – a dignified strip near our place, littered with smaller pedigrees – people would see us coming and reflexively pick their dogs up. Both the other dog owner and I laughed when I said, 'Don't worry, next time I'll pick these two up.' There were times I could even be proud of them, and it was something about there being two. They looked so great together.

'Oh my God, are they from the same litter?' a young woman once asked, out the window of her car.

'Nah,' I said, 'they're just pound dogs.'

'Oh, they're amazing!'

It's only so many years on that I appreciate it as much as I should. Sure, they were wild and troublesome, but their flipside was beauty and light.

As to that first candidate for hostilities in the Most Memorables category, the episode comes to me clearly.

We were lucky enough to live next door to the place where our kids went to day care and kindergarten, and the people who worked there were fantastic. One of the things we loved about our house when we bought it was the sound of children playing next door, and the caregivers. They would say things like, 'Yes, Ethan, come down from there! Yes, *you* – I'm not talking to myself, *buddy*!'

One afternoon, I was collecting Kitty around 4:30, when Belinda, one of the stalwarts of the place, called out to me.

'Hey, Markus! There was just a horrible noise coming

from next door – I think the dogs might have got hold of one of your cats.'

I jumped, grabbed Kitty and ran.

False alarm, but only of sorts.

When we got there, we realized that whatever high-pitched crying had come from our place was Archer. One of his elegant blond ears was covered in blood, and the back porch was splashed with it, too.

I looked at the pair of them.

'Shit, Reuben!'

Reuben was unamused, unmoved.

– *He* asked for it.

Typical Reuben, his face black-brown and deadpan, then sinking a little in shame.

'Look at all that blood!' Kitty called, but there was no real hint of hysteria. In the same way kids are so adept at inventing language, maybe they can also rank scenes of bloodshed. For all I know she was five years old, thinking, Explicit, yes, but no cause for alarm.

I began cleanup of the tiles, the walls and the dog, not necessarily in that order. After wiping Archer down, I applied some pressure to his ear with a cloth, and finally the blood flow stopped, or so I thought.

Much later, when the dogs were inside, Archer gave himself a good shake, and the blood flashed out of his ear again, like someone thrashing a paintbrush. The sight and sound hit everything – the glass, the curtains, the couch, the doorframes, the TV screen, *everything*. It was quite the abstract artwork. The dog had produced a Pollock!

Mika: 'You had to have him, didn't you?'

Me, on cleanup duty, round two, the inside edition. 'Yeah, I really did it this time, didn't I?'

'You sure did . . . I guess you're just waiting for that good luck to kick in, are you?'

'Sure am.'

But again, why were we smiling?

Archer stood beside me with a perfectly timed sad-dog look.

— What? What'd I do?

I grabbed his neck and hugged him.

Sometimes you don't mind the blood.

And so, nearing the end of this chapter, and any ongoing thoughts of Archer bringing me luck?

It never happened.

Frankly, I didn't deserve it, at least with *Bridge of Clay*.

Basically, around every April or May, I make the mistake of telling a few select people my new book will be written by the end of the year. It almost never happens.

In 2011, the stakes were higher.

It had been a tough year for publishers, and Cate, my friend, and my editor at that time, was also head of publishing at Pan Macmillan. By December, she was expecting to be handed the novel, and I still remember when I told her it was over – that the book was nowhere near done. She said she felt like punching me in the face. Honestly, I didn't blame her.

When she came over to give me some tough love and just order me to get it written, a massive dogfight broke out in our yard, and I'm sure I could see her thinking, No wonder you get nothing done – you've made some terrible decisions.

*

That same week, I sat in the backyard for a conference call as part of the board of the Sydney Story Factory. (I was the most incompetent board member they ever had, I assure you. I'm certain there were sighs of relief when I stood down a few years later.)

Halfway through the conversation, the dogs exploded.

Reuben was his vocal self, and Archer gave it back. The epitome of dogs at war. They bounced and leapt through the yard. — Fuck you. — No, fuck *you*. — I'm gonna strangle you. — I'm gonna *kill* you!

All that was missing were knives and busted bottle tops.

One of the other board members cleared her throat at one point. 'You okay there, Markus?'

'Oh yeah,' I replied, 'I'm good. A few wild animals, that's all.' I was just grateful there wasn't any blood.

Later, though, and this was typical, the dogs were back in the house. They'd calmed down, wandered around, and watched the kids do some coloring in. Maybe a bit of reading. Then Archer made himself comfortable, resting his head on Reuben, both of them lying down. His long gold snout was on Reuben's back, and Reuben allowed it, he liked it, and they slept like friends and countrymen. Or better, like sons and brothers.

As for me, I sat beside them, thinking next year would be the year – that *Bridge of Clay* would finally be done – but I was even further away than I thought. Never had I been so deluded.

THE DOG WHO FOUGHT
THE CHAINSAW

Bad fortune hit us that very same December, or as I often put it to people, 'We got Archer thinking he'd be good luck, but as soon as we got him, nothing but bad shit started happening.'

Reuben was nearly two-and-a-half years old.

Archie was about eight months.

On a routine walk, I noticed Reuben limping on his back left leg, but I didn't think anything of it. Like us, dogs have all manner of scratches and bruises, and the way these dogs were pummeling each other, it made sense he could have a small injury. He was normally quick to recover.

As the days went on, the limping was progressively worse. I took him to Paul, our local vet, who was always up for a laugh, and a challenge.

Tallish, curly-haired, and invariably clad in black jeans, a polo shirt and glasses, Paul was the perfect vet for Reuben.

More aptly, he wasn't afraid of him. Where a previous vet had requested Reuben wear a muzzle (I perfectly understood), Paul knew somehow that Reuben wouldn't hurt him, and there was always a dry sense of humor. 'I feel like Reuben and I are connecting,' Paul would say. 'I wouldn't call it *fondness* necessarily, but what do you think – grudging respect?'

'Well, he isn't trying to eat you,' I replied. 'That's a plus.'

'Exactly! Small steps.' Paul would laugh as Reuben manipulated his way into different corners of the exam room. 'Come here, my boy,' and he meant it. He meant his tone of voice. *You're safe with me, it won't hurt as much as you think. You might not like me, but I won't desert you.*

One of Paul's best traits is that there's never a need for panic. Common sense is the first course of action. When I took Reuben to see him about the knee, he gave him a few good stretches. He rotated and felt through the leg.

'Hmmm.'

No one likes a *hmmm* like that one.

He said, 'Look, he's pretty uncomfortable, but unless we get him X-rayed, we won't know for sure how bad this is. It might self-repair, but the fear with big dogs is always the cruciate.'

The cruciate.

Not the prettiest of all the c words in the world, but also not the worst. We remained as casual as possible.

'For X-rays, he'll need to be anesthetized – just so he'll be still enough – so for now, I think just watch him, keep him quiet. No jumping around, no boxing matches with Archer, and we'll see if he improves.'

'Keep them quiet?' I asked.

Paul looked up from the Reub. 'I know, it's a bit of an ask.'

*

As I've said, one of Reuben's better habits was that he never really pulled on walks, and for me that's a nonnegotiable. You can't have a dog bully you on the street (see the start again with Frosty). The dog can't be in charge.

There was, of course, the way Reuben would slow down when Kitty walked him, but as I said, with a second dog in the mix, there could only be more at stake. Mostly, they were fine, but at any moment they might ram each other, or take cheap shots. A fight could break out over nothing. Another dog up ahead would trigger a rapid rise in velocity. I continued walking them together at first, and in the park I let Archer off on his own.

Reuben, it turned out, was fine with it. He was a dog who loved the rough stuff, and could run at good speed for miles, but he didn't mind staying beside me. My theory on that was that maybe he liked the idea that he was chosen to stay close because I loved him more – but that's putting human thoughts into a dog. It's bad enough I give them dialogue for comic effect, but attributing higher-level motivations? Even I know that's a stretch.

It didn't matter; nothing was helping. If anything, his knee was getting worse. At home, we separated them as much as possible, hoping they wouldn't inflame each other, because that's what younger dogs do. And they were siblings now, after all. Siblings fight. It was interesting watching them sleep, on and off, before Archer leaned over and chewed on Reuben's paw.

— Don't touch me.

— Come on, man, let's play.

— Like I'd ever wanna play with you.

— Oh, really? How about this then?

He'd jump up and go straight for the throat.

You can see why we kept them apart.

Mid-January, I took Reuben away for four or five days, to Narrawallee, a place where I worked down the coast. The goal was to make headway on *Bridge of Clay* and give Reuben a break from Archer. It was also to make a decision. If the knee wasn't looking better, it might be time to X-ray. For a month, we'd had him tread lightly, and I continued that for the most part – but there's always that hidden piece of yourself that really just wants an answer. I mean, the dog was still limping. He wasn't improving. At home, I'd compared their legs, and it was easy to see that Archie's, though long and angular, were never going to buckle. Reuben's looked ready to go at any moment.

On the last day of the writing trip, I let him off-leash at the beach. He looked at me, going — You're sure now? You really mean it?

'Go on,' I said, 'go for a run,' and he took that freedom liberally, in every direction imaginable. It was late in the day, waves were rolling. He soared from the mound of sandhills. His grin lit up the evening.

He didn't limp at all as we left the beach, fueled by the thrill and his heart rate, but next day he pulled up sore. As some icing on the cake, after the drive back home, we had a classic city occurrence. Just as I parked on our street and let Reuben out of the car, a skateboarder came graveling past. The dog sprang forward, going after him.

'Reuben!' I shouted. '*Reuben!*'

He stopped, he wandered back.

As I watched, I knew the image. I remembered from watching all kinds of sport when someone has fractured an arm, or wrecked a shoulder, there's that footage of the arm hanging slackly – which was exactly how Reuben returned. That leg hung dead beside him.

Again, I wonder how you judge all that.

Was I totally irresponsible?

I held to the thought that the knee was as good as broken, and we might as well find out for sure. We got the X-rays and the expected. The cruciate ligament was gone.

Paul wouldn't be doing the operation; he's not an orthopedic specialist. The guy who did it was Eugene, and word around town was that Eugene was the man. Eugene knew what was what.

As it turns out, I know a fair bit myself now about reconstructing a dog's knee, both physically and financially. Physically, any vet will tell you it's a great operation, better than a human's.

Financially?

Five grand.

No matter which way you slice it, it's five thousand dollars once you've gone through the X-rays, the surgeon, the painkillers, first recovery, return X-rays (to make sure it worked), and check-ups with your regular vet.

Then, of course, there's the time.

The first few days are obviously the most crucial, then the first week. Then the next *six* weeks. All up, it's six to eight months for full recovery.

The last thing I want to do now is bore you on the topic

of pet insurance, so I'll just come out and say it. We didn't have any. I also don't want to be glib about the value of five thousand dollars. That's a lot of money in anyone's language, and we were lucky we could afford it. It came off the back of our home loan, just as the second knee operation would, and the big one, quite a few years down the road. It's not every day you get a vet bill for $11,897.65, but then, not every dog's a Reuben. For now I'll just say we paid, and I don't regret it for a second.

At the end of January 2012, Reuben went under Eugene's chainsaw. There are many memorable quotes from such ordeals, but a favorite was this one, beforehand, from the surgeon:

'So, basically, we saw straight through this part – *here* ...'

I looked at the forthright diagram.

'Straight through it?'

'Straight through it, yes.'

Poor Reuben, I really felt for him.

I contacted Pat and Clare (you might remember their Reuben lookalike, Thyla). They'd already gone through this themselves, and they lent us their sizable cage, or crate. After constructing it in my office, we let Reuben sit inside, the dog clueless as to what was coming.

Pat and Clare were model dog owners, but they also – and I know they won't mind me saying this – had a dog on the spectrum of vicious. Their devotion to Thyla was consummate, though, and exceptional during her recovery. It was tiring even to contemplate. They told me how they used a rolled-up sheet to pick her up and carry her out for toilet breaks, then the weeks, then months of keeping her quiet.

With two kids, two cats and Archer, we had to make some plans.

Not long before the surgery, I found something near our house. Sometimes it pays to be a street scavenger. (Often, during local bulk disposal days I'll bring something in, and Mika will be rightfully exasperated: 'Oh, come on, not again!')

I'll admit, it's very hit and miss. Mostly miss.

I've brought in bookshelves with terrible slants, and bikes abandoned for good reason . . . but also a homemade toy oven that our children played with for a decade.

When Reuben was close to surgery, I found the top of a table or desk, leaning against a wall. I'd walked past it several times. Underneath, it had a ledge, maybe eight to ten centimeters high, which ran the entire perimeter; I knew that if I placed it facedown, I could create a miniature lawn on it for Reuben. That way, he could live upstairs in my office, which opened out onto the balcony.

Mika and I lugged it upstairs. Next I carried dirt through the house in buckets, and spread it out on the upturned surface. Last, I dug up clumps of grass and planted it into the soil. It actually looked quite good. In months ahead, the grass even grew. I was especially happy because it was practical, and so-called creative people, myself included, aren't known for our common sense. Also, as a kid, I was infamous in my family for being clumsy and regularly hopeless, so I love to get a household job done.

More than all of that, though, it felt like one of those moments when you admit what your animals have done to you. There are acts more telling than coughing up five thousand dollars, and this, for me, was one of them. Certainly not the most intricate of achievements, but it felt like an act of commitment. How much do you love your dog? Well, I built him a lawn on my balcony once, does that count? All these years later, it still does.

I took Reuben in on a humid, cloudy morning, knowing he'd come back much changed. There was the waiting room handover, and the charcoal snout against me. I ran my hand through a last fistful of fur and caught a final blow from his eyes. They glinted in quiet reprisal.

As I drove away, I imagined him knocked out on the operating table, and Eugene sharpening his saw. It couldn't happen to a nicer dog, really, but at the traffic lights, when I stopped, I closed my eyes for just a second, tapping my fingers to my chest.

Let him be okay, I asked, but who did I think I was fooling? He might have been uncommonly breakable, but his mental toughness would soon be unquestioned. It would take a dozen Eugenes and a cavalry of chainsaws to make much impact on Reuben.

Once home, I walked up to the balcony and examined the makeshift lawn. Then I looked at the cage and waited.

THE DOG OF GREATEST SUSPICION

R euben came home with a gigantic shaved patch on one of his sides, a mostly bare back leg, and a drum line of tight-woven stitches. He looked like he'd been in a wrestling match, a boxing bout and a bar fight all on the same night. Other than that, he was fine.

He stayed at the vet the evening of the surgery, and true to Eugene's words, and appearances notwithstanding, he was able to walk next morning. The knee was functional but fragile. The trick was to keep him from running on it.

I lifted him out of my car, and got him into the house.

It was quite a lot of dog.

Stairs were absolutely forbidden, so I carried him up but let him walk the hallway to my office, then out through the doors to the balcony. Immediately he sniffed the lawn. He examined the wooden desk-edge. Then a glance at the guy who'd built it.

He stepped up and gave it the treatment, somewhere

around the middle. Then, and this was typical Reuben, he understood, he walked back inside, past my desk, and lay down on the bed in the cage. There was no complaining, not a whimper, which became standard practice in the years ahead. You could cut Reuben up, you could drug him. You could go within inches of killing him, but all he would do is look at you.

— Really? Is that it?

That said, leave him outside for approximately thirty seconds after his dinner and you'd think he was burning alive.

Of course, when an event of this magnitude happens, you make sure to do everything properly. There was a small pharmacopoeia of drugs to deal with, and we administered them to the letter. (It didn't take long to stop with the pain-killers, though, because Reuben seemed perfectly happy. If he were human he'd have been on the couch, eating chips and drinking beer.)

He took his meals in the comfort of my office.

He'd wander out to his private lawn, then return and settle back in. That's what he thought of knee reconstructions. He ate this stuff for breakfast.

The family visited constantly. Kitty essentially lived in my office, leaning back against the cage onto Reuben. Where her clothes ended, Reuben began. An idyllic picture of exile.

The only visitors considered *personae non gratae* were the cats and especially Archer. Those dogs had been together barely four months, and they would now be separated completely. Any interaction was risky. Reuben would live in my office, and Archer had the rest of the house, and the yard. And essentially the outside world.

The first few days went well, but it wasn't long before we hit breaking point. In situations like this, in a household like ours, something was bound to go wrong. The more careful you are with a family heirloom, the more certain you are to drop it.

Me, I guess I dropped Reuben.

He was not your typical heirloom.

It was the third day of recovery.

Still the most crucial period.

A nasty buildup of fluid was swelling around Reuben's knee, and we thought we should check it with Paul. There was talk of not wanting to move him too much, but in the end we thought it was worth it. I got him down the stairs and loaded him into my car. I won't go into the details about the many-faceted operation of making sure children and other animals were kept clear, but there were a lot. More importantly, in those days, when I traveled with the dogs, I would put the seats down in my car and spread their beds out in the back. Essentially, they took up the whole car except for the two front seats. (It was also not exactly lawful, and I was about to pay the price – in terms of the safety of our dog.)

After settling him in, I was about to close up when I was caught off guard by something thudding to the ground out on the street, and Reuben leapt out of the hatch. He stood, half naked and shivering, his quivering back leg like liquid.

As you can guess, there was quite a bit of swearing; it echoed through the garage. Mika came out as I cursed myself.

'Couldn't keep him together for *three bloody days!*'

Luckily, Paul confirmed there was nothing abnormal with the recovering knee, from both the fluid and Reuben's dismount – and from there I delivered him home again, lumped him back up the stairs, and life went on as normal.

Normal.

I can't help but smile as I write that, because the new normal would slowly evolve. With everything else going on in the house, from Kitty starting school, to Mika's work, my work, Noah, cats – and cats still marking their territory – the dogs, at that point, were easy.

We slowly reintroduced Reuben to exercise. It was a week-by-week proposition. After six weeks there were dog walks happening all over the place. Short ones for Reuben, longer for Archie. I still couldn't let Reuben walk down the stairs, so I carried him up and down, first once, then twice a day. For a few months at least, sometimes there were four dog walks daily.

In the meantime, we wondered.

We knew that Reuben and Archer could hear and smell each other, but were unsure how they'd behave once reunited. Honestly, it's been so long, and I want to be a reliable narrator. For that reason, I can't tell you how it went when we first brought them back together, which leads me to think it must have been okay. If something terrible had happened, I'd remember.

I know we reverted to the pre-surgery days, when Reuben was injured and restricted. In the mornings, I took them both out for a short walk, dropped Reuben home, and took Archer on a proper run.

In terms of Archie's behavior at this time, I would call it something like *handling himself.* I don't think he ever really loved being with other dogs. He loved Reuben and that was it. Other dogs were divided into threatening and non-threatening species. Depending on his mood, or the morning or situation, he would run with them or leave them hanging. If there was contact, he made sure to win. I remember one twilight when he got to work on a pair of slightly undersized Rottweilers. I could see him gnawing at their necks, getting at skin beneath their collars. Their owner, a stout man in his forties with dark, wavy hair, said, 'He plays really well, he knows what to do,' and although I accepted the compliment, I could see the animal within. There was a hard and fast decision made – if it was kill or be killed, he'd choose the former.

The street dog was always inside him.

It just depended how far from the surface.

As the months deepened into winter, the pair of them became familiar again, and again they became formidable. Reuben stayed on the leash, he hit ninety percent recovery, but couldn't quite heal completely. On street walks, it still made more sense to walk them both on my left, but it also came at a price. They could be walking perfectly, happy as you like, before Archer hit out for no reason, and Reuben wasn't having any of it. Walking them early as I did, I'm sure plenty of people were woken by passing acrimony.

I recall one morning in particular, walking up Ocean Street, on the steep part near the bottom. The sun was coming up, and for no reason at all, Archer cut sideways, savaging Reuben in the face. Instant warfare.

Without thinking, I dug my hand in.

I found the closest bit of blond fur and slung him out of

the fray, angry and hard. He looked at me with such injury, seemingly forgetting what he'd done.

— How could you ever do such a thing?

And while his memory was short on his own offenses, it had plenty of mileage on mine. For about a month, he wouldn't come all the way back when I called, like it was me who'd attacked unprovoked.

It came to a head one night in Centennial.

It was dark and the park was empty.

We'd been in the woods and crossed over into the valley. Archie was off-leash, Reuben was on. Everything was fine until it came time to leave, and Archie was especially recalcitrant. When I called, he looked over, maybe fifty meters to the right. He then started a great, looping circle, eyeing me woundedly, suspiciously, on a long, loathsome journey.

Reuben, outraged, beside me. — Oh, come on.

Me: 'I know. Archie, come!'

Archer: — Look, I'm not too sure about that . . .

'Archie, *come.*'

Then the whistle, my three-note signature.

Nothing.

(There's no better feeling than sending out that whistle, the one that only your dog will recognize, and he comes sprinting, steaming back at you – and nothing worse than when he ignores it. The contrast of loyalty and betrayal. A gulf of hurt between them.)

When finally he made it back and sat close by, I motioned to put the leash on, and he instantly jumped away.

We went through that three or four more times, over twenty minutes, and on the fourth I lost my patience, and my nerve, and my love and most of my sanity. I left Reuben and outright chased him. Words clenched into fists, no breaks, no commas or full stops. Just a single exclamation mark at the end: *'Come here you fucking bastard you little shit you pain in the arse!'*

But part-Greyhound is agile and fast.

Up ahead, he loped away, a beautiful streak of light. Mostly what I saw was legs – long, blond legs, and long, gorgeous strides – like chasing a supermodel who'd once been an athlete.

'Arch, you fucking bastard!'

Eventually, he started to tire. I closed the gap and brought him down. I'm sure if anyone was there, it would have appeared quite comical – this guy chasing his dog, then tackling him to the ground, swearing and scourging the whole time. My shoulder was deep in dog ribs, and Archer's face looking injuredly up. We hit the ground quite fast, quite hard. I breathed down shamefully into him, close enough to kiss his snout. I didn't. 'When I tell you to come, it means *come*, goddamn it . . .'

When we got back up, I called Reuben, and we all walked out of the valley. Archer didn't dare touch the Reub, and the Reub looked fiercely ahead.

As the year pulled forward around us, we did what needed doing. Sometimes it felt quite morbid.

It isn't till you think of days and dogs, nights and unslept children, and cats pissing on that rug again, and trying to get some work done, that you realize it's fairly involved. One of my favorite memories is of getting everything finished by about ten o'clock one night, then Mika and I dragging one of the rugs out into the backyard, washing it, scrubbing it, then hanging it to dry on the cubbyhouse. (Wet rugs are hellishly heavy.) The high point of marital romance.

To this day, I see that night sky, a washing machine of stars.

'We must need our bloody heads examined,' Mika said, and I turned to her, quite seriously. Neither of us could have predicted all that still lay in wait for us – our backyard some heinous iceberg. It defied imagination, so it was better to imagine the end.

'When all these animals die,' I said, 'we're not getting any more,' and I absolutely meant it.

part three

REUBEN &
ARCHER'S
GREATEST
HITS

NIGHTMARES BY THE RESERVOIR

There was nothing like having two perfectly fit wild dogs again, ready to resume normal service – or better, renew hostilities. By November 2012, they were back to breach the world again, making up for all that lost time.

But what could they possibly do, you might ask?

How much damage could they actually cause?

I mean, really, they were just two dogs.

Just two dogs.

Such naivety would be understandable if you didn't know Reuben and Archer. Believe me when I tell you. In the years ahead, there'd be brawling and maulings and many things worse. I hate to use the word murder, and more so, murders *plural*. There would be vandalism. A drug run. What we went through with those dogs!

By the time it was all over, they were an unforgettable partnership, exhilarating and frightening. If they'd been a music duo, I see the album cover, looking back at their awful achievements. An inglorious retrospective:

REUBEN & ARCHER'S
GREATEST HITS
2013–17

It started with one of the worst.

As always, there's a backstory, and here it's final recovery.

Memory has always told me it took quite a few months for Reuben's knee to return to 100 percent, but maybe that isn't quite right. Looking back through the sheer mileage of my dog-photo catalogue, there are shots from that year's winter, and they tell a different story. Most prominent was a day down south at the beach, and there they are, the pair of them, locked in usual violence. By the end of the year, it was complete – a purity of menace and force again, more intent than ever before. Especially Reuben. The best player on the team was back, baby, and willing to make it personal. The gleam in his eye said everything.

One thing I haven't mentioned yet is that the owners of problem dogs are most often found in the dark – the gloom of almost-morning, the longer shadows of night. We hide our beasts from the rest of you.

I wonder how many such owners have also used my secondary tactic of taking dogs out in the rain. Too wet for the people with normal dogs? Sounds just right for us. I'd seen enough of Archer going for the throat of slower, smaller breeds, and there'd been a few close calls when Reuben was also in reach. If Archer would start the job, I knew Reuben might easily finish it. The only fortunate counterpoint was that Archer would go for his brother first, to get rid of the competition. I could insert myself between them, grab whichever shoulder I got to, and drag him out of the way. The threat was cut in half.

Only once was there a bigger incident, when Archer went rogue alone. It was early. Centennial and slightly foggy. For whatever reason, a black Lab caught his attention, and I can still see him reaching the slower dog and bringing him down, then letting him go, only to trounce him again – and again – then a fourth time. The owner, oh man, he was furious. I even handed the on-leash Reuben to a Kelpie owner I vaguely knew, and sprinted for Archie and the Lab.

'CONTROL YOUR FUCKING DOG!'

Now there are some words you never want to hear, especially to start your day, but that was what I got when I finally took hold of Archer. I tried apologizing, but the guy was disappearing into the woods, still mouthing off. I didn't blame him.

'I'm so sorry!' I called, but the words were left unheard, almost better remained unspoken.

(Ironically, that same guy still sees me now and says hello once in a while, none the wiser as to who I am and the dog I once owned. He looks a bit like Kojak, a perfectly shaved bald head, and his Lab still alive and well. It's been a while since I've seen him, though, mostly on the footbridge over to Oxford Street that leads to Centennial Park, and the valley: aka the scene of the pummeling.)

After that, it was easier just to keep them away from other dogs in general. I ran them together in solitude. I almost never went down to the valley anymore, and if I did, I always paid. The German Shepherds would round on Reuben again and be faced not only with him, but also his first lieutenant. The park could turn into a street fight; it wasn't quite worth the gamble. So I let them off when no one was around. I stuck to the outer rim, or the quieter depths of the park. Early mornings those fields were empty, but I was always on edge, I was vigilant. The price of wild dogs is freedom. You can never completely relax.

That said, there was also a greater paradox – each day they became more disciplined. Even Archer was growing quite dutiful. Not only would he come when I called him, he would sit within inches of my shoes. Sometimes he'd be slightly touching me. I could feel him against my legs. 'Hey, Arch,' I'd say, and he'd turn to look me in the face, and Reuben would knock him away.

— Move it, shithead.

— Who you calling shithead, *shithead*?!

It could be on, then gone in an instant, the moment I told them to stop. They would sit facing different directions, both upright, both still, their wilderness pent up inside them. Then instantly back to brothers.

And that was always the dilemma.

It took seconds to work their havoc.

A Beagle could simper around a corner, and *bang*. Owners were quite forgiving, especially when I whistled and the dogs recalled immediately. It's the owner who doesn't take it well you fear, and they absolutely have a point. Those incidents were one-percenters, though, but it's the one-percenters we talk about. As I've said before, I too easily forget the vast majority of good times, so for a moment I'll allow it, I'll go there – to the mornings of brightest optimism, and established, impeccable routines.

I remember coming down into the park one early morning and seeing Penny from the local bookshop. Instantly recognizable for her ruler-straight dark hair and perfect posture, she looked up and saw the dogs. They were charging down the track, then shuddered to a halt beside me, because *this is where we stop.* It was a checkpoint to cross the road. As they sat in the fallen leaves, she called, 'Oh my God, Markus, what well-behaved dogs!'

I said, 'Believe me, Penny, we have our days.'

They sat at the ready, half-tilting, waiting for my word, or a gesture.

'Okay,' I said, and they took off.

One of those rain-soaked outings also stands out in my memory. It was an afternoon when a torrential downpour came out of nowhere, flooding Centennial in no time.

As I often do now with Frosty, we ran the outer ranges of the park. On the Reservoir Fields, adjacent to the wide stretch of Oxford Street, the dogs slapped across the ground, making long loping arcs, then flashing, electrically, back together. At one point I stopped and watched them. I pulled my phone out, and like that, a single shot, I took my favorite photo of them ever. It's an image of both raw youth and blinding speed, where Reuben is a textured shadow, and Archie a clean sheet of muscle – midair and fully flexed. You can tell he's turning outward, but aiming to come back in, unafraid of the looming freight train. To this day, I've never taken a better photo. Of anything.

As for where we're getting to, I promise – and it's a foreboding promise at that – we're just about there. (You can't call a chapter *Nightmares by the Reservoir* without a little procrastination.)

First I should explain that it's the truest outliers I fear the most – the one-percenters *of* the one-percenters.

They're the innocent, reckless decisions leading to worlds of unforeseen pain. When you walk an alternative trail, or take a shortcut, or you're ten minutes early or late, you've broken the rules of engagement. Change the playing field or its parameters and there's a chance you'll be met with punishment. Just as I did one Saturday, in January 2013.

I was up a bit faster than usual.

It was still a way off first light when we walked into the park, and for some reason I decided on the Reservoir Fields, which had long recovered from the rain. We never walked there in the mornings.

At the eastern edge of those fields, there's a tired old wire fence, with those diamond patterns, maybe eight feet high, to keep balls from going down the hill. There's another small reserve of grass down there, and steps leading up to the reservoir and its intricate iron barricade. Around the reservoir is a walking track, a fairly common thoroughfare.

When you stand at the edge of those fields, you've got the distant city in front of you and the reservoir at your back. The lower-ground reserve sits just behind your left shoulder. What isn't there anymore is a spindly-looking tree, close to the wire fence, which probably rose to about twice its height. I can't remember anymore the kind of tree it was, maybe a banksia, but what I do remember is the light of the morning in question, or the lack of it. It was the sort of glow where the sun's still tucked in the ground, but the city lights hold firm. The world is never quite dark at the edges of Centennial, both a comfort and slight unease. If we're hurt

A short history of Reuben and Archer:

Brawlers.

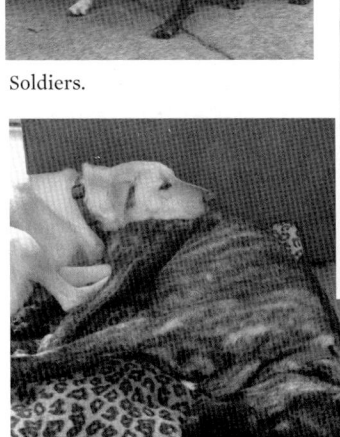

Soldiers.

Team mates.

Brothers.

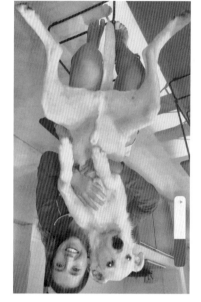

Best of childhood friends: Reuben checking artwork with Kitty and Noah (above);
Archie the comfortable couch (below left); and Frosty – biggest lapdog in the world
(below right).

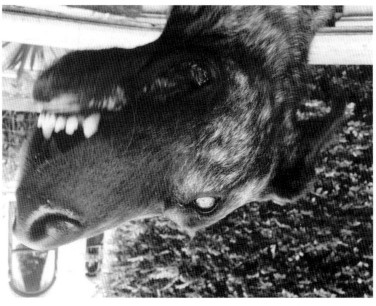

The future: his infamous visage of terror.

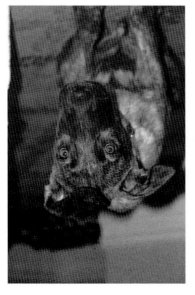

Early Reuben: a sweet little beast.

Bijoux: the ultimate warrior.

PHOTO: WESLEY LONERGAN

Up close and personal with Reuben. He was a lot of dog. At all times. We still miss him terribly.

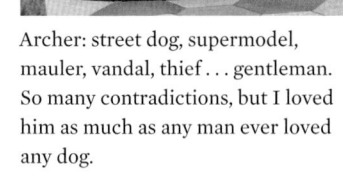

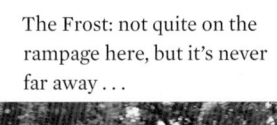

The Frost: not quite on the rampage here, but it's never far away . . .

Archer: street dog, supermodel, mauler, vandal, thief . . . gentleman. So many contradictions, but I loved him as much as any man ever loved any dog.

there might be help close by, but our crimes feel never quite hidden. That morning was no exception.

We walked around the reservoir, a few cars beside us on Oxford Street. Neither dog was on the leash; I could trust them to keep off the road. Up ahead, the fields were ghostly, like a landlocked sea of gray.

We veered instinctively to the wire fence, and I became aware of Reuben's interest in the tree. He trimmed over to it, reminiscent of a wolf, or a jackal. Past injuries were all forgotten. I could sense the ruffled tension. He stood in the classic hunting pose, pressed forward and slightly upward – and the biggest tell of all, a front paw hung slackly in the air. It quivered for a moment, then still.

He looked up into the branches.

The dog was fire-eyed.

Dangerously focused.

Something was definitely up there, either a bird or a bat or possum – and then I saw it. A brushtail was among the branches, up safely enough in the heights.

'Yeah, good one, Reuben, forget it,' I said, 'you'll never –'

He was gone.

He leapt for the tree and was somehow up in the woodwork.

'Holy shit!'

The words had barely escaped my mouth when I realized he'd made it just high enough to haul the possum down, roaring as he did so – and how do I put this politely? The possum wasn't going quietly. It was a great barbaric *yawp* meeting a banshee, then a rolling, tumbling squawking. I can't tell you how long it lasted, but it was significant – half a minute at least (a long, long time in a dog fight, believe me). I got there halfway through. I risked dog jaws and epic

117

possum claws as they fought for life and death, quite literally, in that murky mix of the light.

Next, what might be a strange question, but have you ever tried pulling your dog off something it's trying to kill? Believe me, it's near impossible. You can never quite get hold of them. All the moving parts. Forget those facts about how many muscles it takes for a human to smile, and how many to frown – a dog uses *every* muscle in a fight.

While I grappled and shouted ineffectually, the struggle migrated down the hill, onto the smaller reserve. They were in a sort of arena, or the valley of death itself, and I still couldn't get a handle on him. The frame of his ample musculature, it was lit and overwhelming. He was elbows and gristle, pure force. His heart and mouth, volcanic.

And the possum?

A theater of screeching.

They kept moving, just out of reach.

The next problem, as you might imagine, was *the other one*. A blond presence came hurtling in, as if shot from a close-range cannon.

'ARCHER!' I screamed. 'STAY THERE!'

But of course, there was no stopping him, and up ahead, the ongoing furor.

'REUBEN!'

I reached them and found purchase. I had a hand at the luggage of his neck, the other strapped over his back. Again, I shouted his name, and the voice was not my own. You know those situations, you're deeper, far inside yourself, but also watching on. That long, echoing sound in the distance is you.

Finally, I brought him down.

He coughed up the possum like a fireball. It lay still, spat out, lopsided, like an animal in a crooked picture. Beside it, too close for comfort, were Reuben's prodigious mitts.

How many bones are there in a possum, I wonder? What's beneath that humid fur? What cogs and mechanisms work their watchful, curious eyes? How much does their heart weigh?

Having since looked it up, the bone count is a hundred and twenty-six – and when these particular hundred and twenty-six bones touched the ground that morning, they were soon besieged again. They were set upon instantly by Archer, whose speed was something perverse. I'd never seen such precision, or ruthlessness.

'ARCHER,' I screamed, 'YOU BASTARD!'

Reuben reignited.

I flung him down – 'Stay there!' – and took to Archer with the nub of the dog leash. Again, there'll be the people saying, 'Oh, *there's* a fine example of dog ownership!' But honestly, I really don't care. I hit him once with the girth of the metal, hard in the vicinity of his head, and Reuben (ignoring everything but what was his) came launching straight back in. My God, when would it ever end?!

By some small piece of luck, I capped Reuben's reentry.

'Stay *there*,' I said again, and this time he did. I was then able to get hold of Archer, clip them both to the same leash, and drag them up the steps to the reservoir. When I tied them to the iron bars, Archer nearly took off again, but I clamped him and ripped him down. '*No*, you little shit!' He looked at me like — *What?*

As for Reuben, he stood like a Spartan.

He was blood spots and fur and possum dust.

He looked desperate to finish the job.

*

Next, the heartbreak of aftermath.

I clambered back to the crime scene, fearing death but hoping for a miracle. What greeted me was something worse – a chilling combination of the two.

As I'd hoped, the possum was still alive, lying on his back, with the debris of fur all around him. (Okay, forget how many bones a possum has, the more pressing question is how much fur? I can tell you, it's a lot.)

So yes, to both my surprise and horror, the possum was still breathing, but the breaths were weak and quickening. Dark fur, like a mixed bag of clouds, but the color of earth as well.

Oh shit, I thought, and I looked in his eyes, and they were wide like the glow of a streetlight. His heart was beating too hard for him. I crouched but there was nothing to be done. The claws were half-curled to the sky. Those tiny little creature-hands – and like that, the glow died down.

I saw life climb back inside itself.

I watched the light go out in his eyes.

When you see something like that, it takes a few moments to process, to acknowledge it. I sucked in air and half-darkness. Air and half-light.

As I took in the scene, I noticed there was even more carnage than I thought. It was the end of barely a one-minute war, but the leftovers were something to behold – a promised land of possum fur. It was everywhere, from fence line to final resting place, as dawn was steadily rising, laying light on the dire result. Two dogs stood chained at the reservoir, presiding over what they'd created. Then me, on my knees in the battlefield . . . and terrible as I know this sounds, time was already against us.

Think, I thought, *think*.

Right. I regained composure.

I walked back up to the dogs.

I eyed them with savage sadness, then gave them what I knew of literature at that precise moment in time.

'Arseholes,' I said. 'Fucking bastards.'

Reuben still struggled with fur in his mouth, and I mentioned he might want to choke on it.

For a while we stood together.

I could feel the weight of their breathing.

So began my wrestle with conscience.

It didn't last overly long.

As I pulled myself together, I considered a whole array of possibilities – of what to do next, and how – and arrived at a grim triumvirate.

First, I could keep the dogs tied up and pick up every last essence of possum, from the body to the fur surrounding it. (That would have taken, I kid you not, no less than a couple of hours.) Second, I could grab those hounds of hell, march them from the scene and try to forget this had ever happened. Third, I could return them home and come back to clean up the mess.

The decision was taken from my hands, for as I scoured the perimeter for witnesses, I could see, maybe a hundred meters away, a man coming round the reservoir. Fittingly, he had a baby, and he was using a BabyBjörn carrier – how vengefully goddamn eerie! Imagine standing there with two salivating dogs, both spotted with blood, with the damning evidence below. 'Wasn't us,' I could hear me explaining, and I was the guy in the crime-noir thriller, or at least the slapstick comedy version. I felt suddenly and obviously seen.

Option Three.

I gathered each dog, swearing and clinching tightly, and both of them came out swinging. They wanted more time with the victim.

'No, no – no!' The shout we all cage in a whisper. 'With me,' I said. '*With me.*'

Just before we crossed the six lanes of Oxford Street, I finally dared to look back. I dreaded the dad at the crime scene, but he didn't go down to the reserve. For him, there was no murder. No fight, no burning afterthroat. No fire in the eyes of a dog.

I walked home, bereft and furious.

Muttering, repeatedly.

'What the hell did you have to do that for?'

A static charge remained. It was hackled up in all of us. Their fur still stood on end, the ache of the fight in my arms. Sometimes the dogs looked back again, hoping for a final sniff of it.

'With me,' I said.

With me, with *me*.

A man and his pair of killers.

Like walking a couple of Capones.

At home, I left them in the backyard like I always did post-walk, but today it felt more like a banishment. No doubt they were hoping for another possum out there, for some klutz to slip from a tree.

I sat in the kitchen, moping, still summing up the situation. Should I even go back at all? There would only be more people. What if they started asking questions? (I know, I was hardly Raskolnikov in *Crime and Punishment* – killing his landlord, then spending the rest of the novel paying for it. Realistically, I was more of an accomplice. But still. I felt like a man with possum blood on his hands, and two killing machines out the back.)

Soon Mika came down and I told her the whole sordid saga. The dogs watched on, through foggy breath at the door. Butter would not have melted.

As for the dilemma of going back and effecting a cleanup, we talked the whole thing over, taking criminal sips of coffee. If I was an accomplice to the crime, Mika was an accomplice to the accomplice. As such, this is what we decided.

I wouldn't go back.

Instead, I called the ranger's office and it surprised me when someone picked up. I then described, very calmly, that I'd found a dead possum in a prominent area of the park. I explained exactly where it was – and now, utterly shameless – 'It doesn't look like it was a pleasant death, if you know what I mean. I think maybe a fox got to it, there's a fair bit of mess.' One last swallow now, of guilt and criminality. 'I just wouldn't want someone – you know, someone with little kids – to come past. It might be a bit upsetting.'

Upsetting.

Are you hearing this shit?

The truth is, if it happened today, and with much more firsthand experience of just how much these things are foregone conclusions, I would have left the fur but taken the possum. I'd have hidden it in the thicker grass and come back later to bury it – out of respect, but also the impending

smell. I realize that might be coldhearted to some, and ridic-
ulously sensitive to others:

'They killed a possum, that's absolutely terrible!'

'They killed a possum, it was just a possum!'

For me, at the end of the day, a death is still a death,
a killing still a killing. The majority of humans do have a
conscience, myself included, but we're also complicit in a
world where animals are farmed and slaughtered; we're
hypocrites to be sorry at moments like these. Does it only
count when we're there to see it? Does it only count when
it's not our idea?

Still, I was relieved when the ranger said it would be
taken care of, and thanks very much for the call. (For all I
know he hung up and turned to his sidekick: 'Great, another
possum murder. Wish I got a dollar every time someone
called these in – that fur, it's so damn sticky.')

As for me, I looked outside, to the dogs and their breath
and fog. Like so many TV murders, we'd come to that part
in the plot where the villains get away with it *this time*. And
how exactly did they do it?

Actually pretty easy.

A single anonymous phone call.

A polished performance of lies.

I was alarmed, if only slightly, at how seamlessly I'd done
the job. People might say that we only hurt the ones we
love, but there's a darker truth beneath that, I think, in our
unknown capacity to protect them.

THE YEARS OF MANIACAL
THINKING

Let's face it, it was instinct. If a dog of a certain breed and temperament sees a possum, it's a hunter finding the hunted. There's nothing we can really do.

(Later, I'm sure I'll go into a few details of Frosty's hunting instincts, which for now you can assume to be the same dangling paw as Reuben, but rather than dexterously climbing into trees, it's more a comical leap in the air. He comes stomping back down with his paws, to obliterate anything lurking in the long grass. He's both a predator and a bolter. Truth be told, he makes the other two look like saints.)

As for the high-octane possum incident of Centennial, I remember the leftovers well. The memory of all that noise – the width of it, shrill in my ears. The slow burn of pointless self-pity.

Why? I thought. Why me? Why did I take on these psychotic creatures?

I recall going for a run on my own later that same morning, which was rare. Usually, given time constraints, and keeping two perilous dogs in your care, you take every opportunity to run *them*.

For months there was extra vigilance.

This could never happen again.

But, hey, what can I say?

Shit still happened.

In the immortal words of plenty of notable people, there was plenty more where that came from. To think that we had these dogs and they were still in the prime of their youths. We had such a long way to go.

In terms of setting a timeline, I see that January as twin beginnings. There'd be years of maniacal thinking, and darkest, dauntless comedy. (One thing I've finally learned – when a sustained portion of your life is constantly on the verge of misadventure, it can also be raucously funny.) After all, those dogs might have been complete bastards, but they were also beautiful darlings. They were like your teenage sons. When the madness stopped and the punishment or recovery period was negotiated, it was only a matter of time before the laughter set in.

They were forever entertaining.

Especially when they were bad.

First up, the day of the drug run.

Yes, drugs.

Let's just say it's not that often you go to the vet four times in a single day and have both your dogs' stomachs pumped.

Given we live near our local primary school, for years we sporadically had kids dropped in by parents in the mornings, or they'd stay in the afternoons. It was something we really enjoyed, although we had to watch those dogs. There's the unpredictability of animals *and* children, so it was safer to keep Reuben and Archer in my office.

It was late April, which meant the cats were due for vaccination, and Reuben would go in for a Pentosan shot, to keep his now reconstructed knee, as Paul would say, well lubricated. I drove the cats down first (a meowathon in the car), and returned later with Reuben, who'd been limping slightly on the knee. For added comfort, Paul prescribed some anti-inflammatories and dropped them into a zip-lock bag, and everything should have been fine.

When we returned home that afternoon, Archer was already up in my office, and I took Reuben in to join him. The tablets were still in my pocket, and I still can't tell you why I threw them onto my desk in their neat little plastic wallet. There might have been sixteen or eighteen of them, I don't know, shaped like dice, only flatter, and light brown. I finished off some work, left the dogs on their ample beds (they took up serious real estate on the floor), and went back downstairs to the kids. There was jumping on the trampoline, and oranges cut into quarters. When the kids and parents were gone, however, maybe an hour later, I walked back upstairs, opened my office door and found the zip-lock bag in pieces, all of it wet with saliva.

Immediately, I closed my eyes.

Both dogs were content on their beds.

'Oh, shit,' I said.

They each looked up, simultaneously.

'You ate all the anti-inflammatories!'

I searched for a solitary remnant. Nothing.

— You mean you didn't want us to? They almost looked at each other and shrugged. — We just assumed. Or else why would you have left them there? Up high on the desk like that? Unguarded? I mean, what did you expect?

Again, we formed a jury.

Both Mika and I assumed it was most likely Archer, the noted greedier of the two. It was well after dark but Paul was still open, so I rang him and explained. I told him we suspected Archie, and he suggested I bring him down. After a fairly judicious pause, he said, 'We might have to pump his stomach.'

To this day, I have no idea what's involved in a human stomach-pumping, but the reality here was that Paul had a kind of mixture that he forced down Archer's throat – motivation to cough up the goods. Also, he'd laid down sheets of newspaper, so in accordance with Murphy's Law, and Archer being Archer (greedy but quite weak-stomached), he threw up immediately and copiously, everywhere *but* on the newspaper. After which Paul, God love him, got started. He examined what Archer had left us.

Soon he peered up.

Not quite the look I wanted.

'Markus, I hate to tell you this, but I'm not seeing much evidence of the tablets here . . .' He was plastic-gloved, still crouching, the light glinting off his glasses. 'Do you think there's a chance Reuben ate the tablets, not Archer?'

How could I not laugh? 'You do realize this is the third time I've been down here already today, don't you, Paul?'

Paul was typically wry, using the newspaper for initial cleanup. He waved me away from helping. 'Well, we do all get on pretty well.'

I shifted my gaze to Archie, who looked dazed, nauseated and confused.

'You,' I said, 'come with me.' He gave me a mournful glance. 'Don't worry, now it's Reuben's turn,' which did seem to cheer him up. 'All good to come straight back down?' I asked Paul.

'It's a date.'

He was crumpling up the news.

Then Reuben.

Hard-as-a-coffin-nail Reuben.

Let me just put it this way:

With Archie, Paul likely didn't even need the dreaded powder. Reuben, on the other hand, walked in and immediately smelled a rat. Knowing that Paul was up to something even more diabolical than normal, he refused to open his mouth. When finally we got it open, he swallowed the package gamely, then looked at Paul with bemusement.

— Is that it?

Paul let out a 'Hmm.' He regarded the dog as he often did, that blend of affection and humor. 'Most dogs do refund this stuff quite quickly, so let's give him a minute.'

One minute, two – nothing. Soon we'd have to turn the radio on, although Paul was good company enough. He would often tell me about books he was reading (he was a big Justin Cronin fan back then), and I was happy to hear all about them.

When a third minute passed, Paul gave Reuben a second helping. Mouth open, shove down the powder – again, nothing, only this time there was no perplexity from the dog, more just a mild resentment.

— I know what you're trying to do here, and just so you know, it's not gonna work.

By the third time, Paul was talking statistics. There was a woman who did the weather on TV, who also brought her dog to Paul. Apparently, it was her leathery little Schnauzer who'd so far had the strongest tolerance for the powderworks.

'If Reuben gets through this one,' Paul said, 'and needs a fourth instalment, he'll officially hold the record.'

I wondered for a moment if there was a medal or plaque. What would you even write on it?

'Well, it's a proud day for all of us,' I said.

Paul was quite intrigued, really mulling it over. 'Not a bad record to have, I reckon.'

'Well, he's not winning any prizes for his looks, is he?'

'Come on, Markus, that's a bit harsh. There's definitely some rustic charm there, look at him.'

We looked.

Reuben had pressed himself against the wall, like a binge-drinker trying to stay upright. Pure determination. God, I loved him a lot. He looked at us somewhat bleary-eyed. Again, he seemed to revive, though, and Paul had seen enough. 'Well, Reuben,' he said, 'I have to hand it to you. You're a dog with an iron will, and a cast-iron stomach to match.'

With the fourth sack of powder breaching his throat, Reuben finally faltered, but first he stood proudly, defiant. It was *he* who made the decision, and he who stood, legs splayed. — All *right*. Then steadying. — All right, but just so you know, I'm only doing this now because I want to. Nothing to do with you.

With a final display of belligerence, he took a single step

forward and produced. When he was done, Paul got to work again, examining – a little too enthusiastically if you ask me, but a man has to love his job.

Me, I gave Reuben a hug, I couldn't help it, his neck like a miniature grizzly. 'Anything down there, Paul?'

An air of disappointment. 'Well, I hate to say it, but not really.'

Reuben just looked at me glumly.

— Thanks for nothin'. Let's go home.

That year brushed by like they all did, or at least how they did for us:

Love and comedy and violence.

As with all stories, there were side characters, like the smaller dogs, acting tough. I understand that a small dog's bark is its only weapon, but some were taking it too far, and the reactions were polar opposites.

Whenever they were feverishly barked at, Reuben would play unaffected.

— Not even looking at the little pissant.

Archer wasn't quite so benevolent.

There was one dog, I don't know exactly what it was, but it was small with that angry-face look. You know the ones, the jutting jaw, and teeth like medieval torture devices. An old couple used to walk him around our neighborhood, and not that I didn't have problems of my own, I always felt kind of sorry for them; that dog was pure ferocity. His bark would shriek and echo. It was like he was packing a megaphone. I'm sure what he was trying to say was — Hey you guys, I'm just scared out of my mind here and I'm only little, so could you please keep your distance?

It certainly didn't come out like that, it was more like *ready to rumble*:

— COME HERE, YOU SONS OF BITCHES, I *DESPISE* YOU! TAKE ONE STEP CLOSER AND I'LL BUST YOU *UP*!

I'll always remember the man's beige pants, his wire-rimmed glasses, the unkempt hair beneath his hat. The forbearance of the woman, putting up with it all, wincing as the dog blustered on.

Reuben would take no notice, of course, but every time we walked by, Archer watched intentionally, almost licking his lips. By the end he'd be looking up at me, pleading his silent case.

— Come on, man, just once. Let me off this leash *just once*, that's all I ask, I'm begging you!

It wasn't hard to know what would happen.

I got a taste one day at home.

Our neighbor, Iska, with whom we shared a path, had a sweet but headstrong little Papillon called Isabelle, shortened to Izzy. Now, nothing against Izzy and her prim, upper-class stature, and those delicious, floppy ears, but she did love barking at us whenever we walked past. She would shout from her little courtyard above – and sometimes, when Iska let her out, she'd leave small, dainty gifts at our front door, and once or twice, she pissed at the bottom of our gate.

Now, I know. I could have been an adult, I could have been assertive and had a quiet word with Iska, but I didn't really want to, not yet. I thought I'd wait till it became an actual problem, but really, I should have known. A dog marking another dog's territory? That's a declaration of war, and Archie was the dog to deliver. He pined for retribution, it was obvious.

A Saturday afternoon.

I brought the dogs home from a walk, unclipped them, and left our gate open for just a moment – they always went straight in – but on that day, a moment was all it took. Izzy pranced down the path, delivering a tirade, and Archer swept past me, grinning. I'd never seen his mouth open so wide. He couldn't believe his luck.

'Archie,' I called out, 'shit!'

Like a blond, careering runaway, he mowed her down in two seconds flat. Then, as soon as she found her feet again, wondering what in the name of *French fucking champagne* had just happened, he skidded to a halt near the top, and came screaming back down toward her, trampling her on his way home.

As poor Iska was having heart palpitations, Archie trotted past me.

— Told you I was going to get her.

He did all but smack his paws together, like someone saying, 'Job done.'

Me, I started peace talks.

'Oh man, sorry, Iska, I'm so sorry . . . Is Izzy okay up there? Bloody Archie, the big bully!'

But I have to hand it to Iska. She was eccentric, but she also had a good understanding of dogs. She was very quick to forgive, but she would never, ever forget. Even years later, she'd say, 'Ooh, that naughty Archie,' whenever she saw him. But she'd smile, she didn't resent him. 'You know, Izzy still remembers . . .'

I bet she does, I thought.

And while I can't fully endorse Archie's methods that

day, I'll allow him this much: Izzy never pissed near that gate again, and one thing was perfectly clear. When it came to suburban warfare – from street fights to scraps, to dealing with smaller, insolent pests – I'd have backed Archer in almost anything.

VANDALS

In those years of outbreaks and lunacy, there was also thievery and vandalism, which leads to a secondary question.

What caused the greater mayhem?

To be honest it was probably the thievery, but the vandalism was more spectacular. The commentary was mostly identical. It was usually 'Bloody Archie!' We blamed him for almost everything.

In the end I've realized that dogs can mostly be categorized like humans. Personalities range from quiet through to bombastic, submissive through to savage, reliable to selfish. Even bathroom strategy varies. (Reuben was definitely a bush boy, seeking privacy, but Archer – shy and sweet as he presented himself – was something of an exhibitionist. His ideal toilet would have been a professionally mowed football field and a stadium of cheering fans. Never mind that he'd look embarrassed, he'd be enjoying every minute. He was also what I'd call a wandering shitter, or a Hansel – leaving a breadcrumb trail behind him. It offered clues to his gift for troublemaking.)

And troubles were surely lurking.

Toward the end of 2013, I noticed Reuben limping again, this time on his other back knee. I instantly knew it was gone. We booked him in, we got it done. Again, the dogs were separated, and after a small stint upstairs in my office (including a failed synthetic lawn this time on the balcony), we kept him downstairs with Archer; Reuben just stayed in the crate. I carried him down the steps to the yard for toilet breaks. They'd grown up a bit more by then, so after the requisite first six weeks, we could walk them slowly together. There were no shenanigans on the leash. Both dogs walked deadly straight. In the house, when it wasn't Kitty or Noah leaning against the cage, it was Archer – blond on brown through the metal. It was something I loved to be around.

Don't get me wrong, it was still a pretty arduous six-to-eight-month process, but the second knee recovered quicker. Now whenever someone asked the stock question about their breeds, I'd point to Reuben and say, 'Well, that one's a two-dollar dog with two five-thousand-dollar knees.' He was a cyborg animal if ever there was one, or dog with a dash of terminator.

In 2014, we bought a shack down the coast in Bendalong, as a place to work in solitude, but also for trips with the family. It's a small community of mostly rundown vacation homes and a sprinkling of people who live there. It's where we met lifelong friends, especially Angus and Masami, our closest neighbors, who were permanent residents at that time. We got on well for many reasons, and their children are similar ages to ours. Masami's a constant generous spirit, and Angus is your typical curmudgeon with a heart of gold, and also the perfect surf friend – always keen and on time. If surfing toward evening, he's also the sort of guy who'll catch his last wave before you, but then stay in the deep water and wait. When the light fades, and it's starting to feel what surfers and ocean swimmers call *sharky*, that's the guy you want there with you. He'll never let you down.

But what does that have to with dogs, and our dogs in particular?

I think it's in the attitude.

When Angus first came over, with vegetables from Masami's garden, he saw the dogs out the back and grinned. (He's also a bit of a shit-stirrer, Angus, fairly tall, with short but feathery hair. He's spent time as a pilot in New Guinea, and also as a jackaroo – he's seen a lot of the world, and knows a thing or two about animals.)

'Those hounds look pretty handy,' he said. 'Can I go out and say hello?'

Mika was quick to warn him. 'Well, they might attack you is the thing.'

He grinned even bigger. 'Really? Nah, I'll be right.'

As he walked to the back sliding door, we made sure Kitty didn't go out with him, because Reuben, especially, might get his back up.

Sure enough, Angus walked out and talked to them, not an inkling of fear in his aura. 'You, you bastard,' he said to Reuben. 'Yeah, I get it. You're a big tough brooding bastard.'

Then he turned to Archer. 'And you – you've got a head like a kangaroo. I'm calling you Kangaroo-Head.'

Angus has a knack for nicknames, but they're not always politically correct, let's say. His favorite later on was for Archie, who he called the Gay Dingo, and it stuck. Even the most culturally diverse and law-abiding of our friends would shrug their shoulders and laugh. 'You know,' they'd admit, 'it kind of suits him.'

While we're here, a quick note on south coast kangaroos.

As you might know, they often frequent people's front lawns down there, or beach car parks, and sometimes the beach itself. (I recall surfing one afternoon with Angus at a break best accessed by hiking, about two-and-a-half kilometers away. When I was getting out of the water, I saw a kangaroo outwit a fox by jumping out into the tide. It made me realize, as if I didn't know already, what goes on out there in the bush. There are miles of it behind the coastline.)

As you can imagine, we had a few dogs of our own who would go for the kangaroos, but again, they were also trainable. They weren't kids anymore, they listened. Reuben, as spiritual leader, would go — Right, got it, and Archer duly followed. I can't remember anymore how long it took, but one of my lasting memories of those dogs is walking them off-leash down Pine Street, or Bendalong Road, and they wouldn't even look at the kangaroos either side of them . . . Frosty, so far, is the opposite; see previous note on personalities.

*

In so many ways, they were great dogs, Reuben and Archer, but there were instincts they still couldn't ignore. Sure, I could train them off kangaroos, but let's not forget the possum, or the ever-present threat of one-percenters. Also, it's often the big problems that are sorted out while the smaller ones eat away at you from below – and Archer was consistently down there. If eating was an event at the Olympics, he'd have likely been a medalist, and he was also the ultimate instigator.

Within those two traits, there was a scoreboard of terrible habits. Baiting, chewing, stealing. It wasn't that he committed these things often, but when he did, he did them hard. If he chewed a book, it was your favorite book. (I'm still pissed about the spine he ruined of my hardcover of *Barbarian Days*, the great surf memoir.) Then exercise equipment – the sort of thing with resistance bands and hard plastic handles – he could chew them just enough that even after you taped them up, they could snap again when you least expected it. The handle would ricochet off the walls and hit you in the face. If he disgraced himself in the park again, giving some poor unsuspecting dog a drubbing, he'd be dragged straight home and left there, while Reuben was taken back out. Things were fine for 364 days of the year, but God help you on the 365th. On that day he was like the friend who shakes up a can of soft drink and opens it in your face.

To be fair, there'd been plenty of smaller crimes and misdemeanors from both dogs up to this point. Digging up fertilizer in the backyard for one thing, and ravaging the bag. Two snoutfuls of Dynamic Lifter isn't the most pleasant thing in the world, and it doesn't do much for their intestines. But it was Archer who made the best thief. He had the skills and motivation, and the right amount of cunning.

He could plant his considerable front paws up on the kitchen counter and eat whatever was left there. The remnants of a bowl of oatmeal? Licked clean, in silence. The bowl wouldn't even move, polished off so expertly that Mika or I would come along and ask, 'Did this bowl actually get used?' Only once did he leave just the smallest bite of wet wheat on the edge of the table, and we went, 'Ah-ha! Archie, we caught you this time!'

His list was quite extensive.

Butter left out to soften – gone.

The last two Tim Tams – pickpocketed from the packet.

An entire apple crumble – *disappeared*. Mika stood in the kitchen, wondering if she'd even baked it. 'It was right here! Look, there's nothing left! Not even a crumb. You'd think it never existed!'

But all of this was nothing.

Nothing compared to the chicken.

At the time of writing, my family consists of two vegetarians and two mostly vegetarian meat-eaters; that is, we'll eat meat once, maybe twice a month, and also when it's put in front of us. In April 2015, though, we were all still in the latter category, and the plan was roast chicken on Easter Sunday; Halina and Jacek were coming for lunch. I took it out of the freezer on Saturday morning and left it to defrost, and we hurried out, as usual, for kids' sport. For whatever reason, I'd already unwrapped it, and it sat on a plate in the sink –

Cue, Archie.

Reuben was likely smart enough to know what raw chicken could do to his system, but Archer most definitely wasn't. With the length of his legs and his snout, he must have planted those front paws and gathered up the chicken. When we got home, we found it mauled on the wooden floor, like the corpse of a frozen football. Archer was circling away from it, guilty as hell. The look on his face said it all.

— How did that bird get there, I wonder?

There were all sorts of accusations, and he slunk away like a scolded child, while I sorted through what was recoverable.

'You're not still going to cook that, are you?' said Mika. She knows me far too well.

'Well, he didn't eat *all* of it. Not a word to your mum and dad tomorrow, okay?'

It took her a moment to realize I was joking.

What wasn't a laughing matter hit later that afternoon, and most of the following week, due to Archer's delicate stomach. The first evidence was the most macabre expulsion ever witnessed in our house – half on the floorboards of my office, half on the rug in there. That rug. It had seen everything from cat urine to dog shit to kids' vomit, but this was something else. I melted fairly quickly.

'Oh, Arch,' I said, 'you okay, buddy?'

It was the sorriest I'd ever seen him.

We headed down the coast next day, and when the infection wouldn't self-regulate, we met Carrie and Matt, the excellent vets in Milton, whom we've now seen three times at last count. Second was for Reuben to get some stitches out, and last was rushing him in one night, wondering if he had a tick I couldn't find, but it was cancer inching through him. We'll get to that one later.

*

Which brings us to the night of vandals.

Again, my office was the setting.

I remember it was a Friday evening, and there were kids in our backyard, trampolining, and their parents in the kitchen, drinking, probably out of necessity. The dogs were in my office, in their Hilton of rotten bedding. We heard an ongoing commotion, till someone said, 'What are they *doing* to each other up there?'

Mika asked if I wanted to check.

'Nah.' I thought I'd live dangerously. 'They'll settle down.'

It lasted another five minutes or so, and I thought we were pretty safe, given there wasn't much they could destroy – in theory. I'd forgotten I'd just had a box of *Book Thief* reprints delivered. Six books in a cardboard box.

Later, when everyone left, I went up to my office, opening the door to a snowfield of books and paper. Almost unphotographable, such was their accomplishment. It was everywhere: ripped-up bubble wrap, annihilated pages, and my favorite detail of the lot – in one of the books, the author photo on the inside cover was scalped right down to the eyebrows. In others it was torn to shreds, committed, it seemed, with intent. — Here, get this into ya!

'Oh my God,' I whispered, in one of those eerie, quiet cataclysms. Small things, we lose our minds. The big ones, we remain quite peaceful. (I was far angrier about the small tear in *Barbarian Days*.)

For a moment I simply watched – ruefully, open-mouthed – amazed at these infernal creatures. So blissful among their rubble.

'Um – hey, Mika?' I finally called. 'You want to come up here?'

Her voice carried up the stairs.

'Oh, no, do I really want to?'

The kids came up as well, and we regarded the blizzard before us.

'Look at your author photo!' Mika laughed. 'One of them ripped right through you!'

'Do you have to say that so cheerfully?'

Strangely enough, I love that memory now, for a wide variety of reasons. For a start, it wasn't a drug run, and the cleanup would be pretty straightforward. Mostly, it's remembering how they just sat there, paws stretched out before them, especially Archer, like a prince in his kingdom of anarchy. Or Nero debauched in Rome.

And Reuben now watching me sternly.

— Where the hell have you been, anyway?

Then Mika measuring the damage.

She looked from dog to dog, and me, and made her fitting summation. 'I guess everyone's a critic, huh?'

It was time for them to be fed, and everyone left the room, children and dogs included. I closed the door behind me. Sometimes, at least for a while, all you can do is leave it. Pretend it never happened.

the two worst moments, part i:

THE DOGS WHO BIT THE
PIANO TEACHER

The title says it all.
   Everything led to this.
There was, as it were, an incident.

First, in the years leading into 2016 and '17 (when the two
worst moments occurred), our family leaned steadily toward
less meat-eating, and less dairy, and more into vegetarianism.
It had everything to do with animals.

   The word *fraught* comes to mind on this subject, and like
almost every other issue these days, we increasingly seem
to take sides. For those at the extremities, battle lines are
drawn:

   Meat-eaters are heartless savages.

   Vegans are militant snowflakes.

   My promise is not to bombard you with any of that; it's
not what this book is. Just as it's not a how-to-train-your-dog

guide – we're about to get into *piano teacher attacks*, for God's sake – it's also not a responsible-eating manual. For starters, how do you talk up vegetarianism on moral grounds when you feed your pets a diet of mostly meat? Second to that, how many animals are killed to keep a single dog alive in its lifetime?

And the questions keep on coming.

Can an animal-lover eat a steak?

Can a vegan annihilate a cockroach, or celebrate the death of a mosquito? ('Gotcha, you little bastard!')

Either way, when you're thinking about it all – the city, the country, people's livelihoods, the welfare of animals and the planet – it's not that easy to feed your family, let alone your pets, with a restful mind. In the end, Mika and I have sought an inner common sense. We realize it's hard to rail against animal consumption when you feed your animals *animals* . . . and, you know, a piano teacher every now and then. (It's taken a long time to see the funny side, believe me. Actually, no, I still can't.) And what do they say about the road to hell being paved with good intentions? We were definitely about to find out.

Which brings us to our moment.

March 2016.

Our kids had both been doing group piano lessons at the Australian Music School in Randwick, on the other side of Centennial Park. They were taught by the glorious Lindi, or *Miss Lindi*, if you want to keep it professional.

What can I say about Lindi? She was just one of those teachers. Children loved her, adults loved her. Especially when the kids were still quite young, us parents would sit in class with them and watch her go to work. In black pants, an AMS T-shirt and impossible ringlets of dark brown hair, she was a wealth of generosity and energy. She was always quick to laugh, maintaining endless wonder for the myriad oddball statements and off-topic monologues as the kids crowded round her keyboard.

'Franklin!' she'd say. 'What have you got there? A space-ship, I see.' She must have seen that bloody spaceship three hundred times, but she was seeing it again for the first time. 'And what about you, Julia? Any news this week? No? Okay, let's get to work.'

Which was the other great trait of Lindi's. She could keep her kids on track. She expected something from them, and when someone mucked up in her class, they never mucked up for long. As I've said, there wasn't a child or parent who didn't love her, and we always made special efforts on end-of-year cards and gifts for her.

And then what happened, happened.

Thankfully, it's not every day your dogs bail up a charismatic music teacher who also happens to be the nicest person on Planet Earth. Trust me, once is bad enough, it's awful. But of course, it was *awfuller* for her.

They were lucky to be alive after this incident, I'm certain of it, because they did shorten Lindi up, and one of them did bite her. (I'm not even going to soften it with the word *nip*.) It was a testing moment for all of us. I've felt the guilt of failed responsibility many times in my life, but this was sickness-in-the-stomach stuff, absolute rock bottom. It was a sodden Monday morning.

I was coming home from a short but intense book tour in

America for the tenth-anniversary edition of *The Book Thief*.
It was ten cities in eleven days on both sides of the country,
and the Midwest. The readers were magnificent – extraor-
dinarily open and friendly – but the travel was a logistical
nightmare. Almost every flight was delayed, and I'm still
shocked I made it to every event. Mostly, I ate once a day,
which was breakfast at the airport. Gratifying but not so
glamorous. The tour finished in Miami, and all that stood
between home and me was a five-hour flight to L.A., then
sixteen hours to Sydney. Piece of cake.

When you're flying into Sydney, you typically expect
sunshine. My favorite landing story still comes from a beautiful sunny morning a few years earlier. I was sitting next to an
older couple from Cleveland who were constantly asking me
where the casino was and could they walk there from their
hotel. The woman was particularly dour, and when I pointed
out the Opera House through the window, she drawled,
'*Looks kinda small . . .*' I couldn't help laughing, I loved it.

On that morning, however, mid-March in 2016, the skies
were unforgiving. The rain was cantering down. I took a taxi
with that familiar itch in my heart, where you just can't wait
to see everyone.

I walked in the door around 10 a.m. The kids were both
at school. I was in the kitchen. About three seconds after
dropping my bags, Mika said, 'Hey, I have to tell you something,' and between us, instant gravity.

I knew it wasn't something good.

And I knew, without doubt, it was the dogs.

This was how it usually worked with Lindi.

First of all, most kids who did piano lessons at AMS had

Noah and Archie: second borns in all their glory.

Although Reuben thought he was food when we first brought Noah home, he learnt immediately that he was family – to be loved and completely protected.

Noah and Arch: walks in winter after school.

Mika tending to Reuben after his second knee reconstruction.

Another day in the park:
Mika and Archie.

Kitty and her boys.

Archer's complex relationship with literature . . . reader (above); connoisseur (below left); destroyer (below right). Note the vandalised author shot among the carnage – although Reuben gave him plenty of help.

A torrential afternoon: my favourite
photo of Reuben and Archer ever.

Kitty and Reuben's last great moment in
the sun . . . saying goodbye and they didn't
know it.

Reuben, near the end. The more life
beat him up, the handsomer he got.

Mika and Reub – last morning.

Remembering the good times,
the great times!

Archie getting used to life on his
own – indulging in a game of
Monopoly.

Arch, post-fires: like walking on the
surface of the moon.

Not that Archie and Brutus actually became friends or anything . . .

Sinking dogs are tragic and golden,
as are the kids who love them.

Archer. My sentinel – and remains so
even now as my screensaver, watching
over me while I work.

Natural states of the Frost:

Stick fiend.

Sweetheart.

Not so photogenic.

Madman.

What's left? They are ours. We are theirs.
There's not a dog I want to forget.

a one-hour group class once a week, then a half-hour private lesson on a different day, in one of the smaller rooms of the school. For us, Lindi came to our house instead, at eight o'clock on Monday mornings. (One of her daughters was in the accelerated program at Kitty and Noah's school, and Lindi would drop her there and come to our place. Or sometimes her daughter came in with her.)

Given Reuben and Archer were taken out first thing in the morning each day, when Lindi came on Mondays, I was already back home and the dogs were outside in the yard. It was such a failsafe routine that we told Lindi to just come straight in when she arrived – and there, the imminent danger.

On the day in question, Mika took the dogs out early and the rain hit hard, mid-walk. She trudged on, brought them home, dried them off, and they were in the house from around 6:45. She would put them back out after an hour or so, or shut them into my office.

As it goes with children sometimes, though, you have *mornings*, and this was one of those mornings. Cereal spilled on the floor. Fights and almost fisticuffs. Frustration. Shouting. Tears, lost uniforms, even though you laid them out the night before. 'I mean, how did it manage to disappear in the last five minutes? Just put something else on!'

'I can't, I'll get in trouble.'

'All right, I'll write you a note . . . and you can't wear those shoes. Get your gumboots.'

'I'm *not* wearing gumboots.'

And so on.

*

At 8 a.m., Mika was still upstairs dealing with Noah, when Lindi came in as always, probably quicker than usual, avoiding the rain, and inside, in the distance – dogs.

And not just any dogs.

They were *our* dogs, of certain reputation.

I see them in slow motion, their legs and heaving chests. Blond and brown, the ignition of eyes. Flapping jawlines from the force of movement. The oncoming violence of teeth.

They erupted down the hallway.

When Mika heard the scream, she knew.

She clamored downstairs to find Lindi cornered near the front door, and the dogs watching her. Jesus, can you imagine Reuben? He was the very visage of terror, I'm sure, with the intent of full-blown barbarism. Proximity was barely a meter. Then Archer, positively hackled, his spine alight with fur. Ready. *At* the ready.

When Mika ordered them away, they left immediately. Their work here was done. Someone had entered the house, they'd scared the absolute hell out of her. They'd given her due warning of what would happen if she took a single step further.

They were put outside right away.

Lindi said she was fine, and Mika couldn't even tell at first if she'd been bitten. They breed 'em tough in the music world, believe me.

Again, Lindi insisted, 'I'm fine, I'm absolutely fine.'

It was the shock talking, because Lindi, in fact, was not fine. She proceeded to our cheap plug-in keyboard, as Mika asked her again if the dogs had got to her, and Kitty, who was nine at the time, cried, 'Oh no, not again!'

Yes, you read that correctly.

Not the words you want coming out of your child's mouth when your dogs have abandoned their manners in the worst possible way. Apparently, she was referring to the general idea of things going wrong with our animals, and not specifically *maulings*.

For Lindi, it can only have been the adrenaline.

She was reeling, revolving within.

'I'm fine,' she kept saying, 'it's fine, these things happen.'

She was determined to start the lesson, and the complete truth only came out afterward, as she was leaving – there was a wound beneath her shirt. She'd been bitten by a charging dog, all right. She just didn't know which one.

Even as Mika persisted in asking, out of concern, and to accept whatever the consequence, Lindi was adamant; everything was good. (Again, someone of her generosity will only want to smooth things over.)

But nothing that morning was smooth.

Punishment comes in various ways, and my first order of business was to make the call. I can't remember if I opened my office door (where the dogs had since been relocated; it was pouring outside), but somehow I don't think I did.

What I do remember is walking into our bedroom – the very same place where Mika had once called, 'Hey, I think I found us a dog!' – and placing my bag down onto the bed. I shoved a knee in the ribs of the mattress, then looked at my phone and dialed. The severity of that ring, when you dread the sound of the answer. Sometimes it's truly a death knell, or like that final line of *The Snows of Kilimanjaro*, where the woman can't hear the distant howling hyena for the beating of her own heart.

Lindi picked up.

My stomach was sunken but sideways. It was warped by the force of ineptitude, and by guilt and pity, culpability . . . and that's just naming a few.

Her voice felt far away.

I clenched my eyes when I heard it.

'Hello?'

the two worst moments, concluded:

BARBARIANS ON THE STAIRS

O utside, the howling rain.
　　My knuckles around the phone.

Lindi was nothing but gracious, accepting my constant apologies, and our offer to pay her doctor's bill. (I know. Not sounding good.) Most troubling of all was that she ended up with two stitches at the hinge of her elbow. That always raises the stakes. Stitches make it real and *vicious*.

When she asked if the dogs had done anything like this before – on account of Kitty's exclamation – I told her they were definitely on the spectrum, but they'd never bitten anyone. I described how we managed them, how we loved and took care of them – that they were pound dogs we'd taken in, that we'd saved them from death row, you know, really laying it on. After all, this was deadly serious. Their lives were on the line. Whether they deserved to live was debatable, but I wasn't too keen to risk it.

Before I spoke again, I weighed the price of a child's heart, which at first was the heart of Kitty. Reuben, especially, was like a brother to her, and putting him down was inconceivable. But then Noah as well – those dogs preceded his memory. Their lives were embedded into his. He walked and sometimes fed them; his bedtime stories were so often had with a dog paying equal attention, or beside him, lying on the floor. I don't want to say it would have destroyed those kids because we can never account for the resilience of children, but testing that out right now felt almost too cruel to be true. To be avoided at all cost.

That said, I swallowed and showed at least a few different sides of human nature. I was simultaneously stoic and cowardly, and calculating in the worst possible way.

'Lindi, I totally understand if you need to tell someone about this. If you need to report it to the police, I won't blame you, I'll totally understand.' (I knew full well that these sorts of incidents are reported to council, not the police. Unless the attack is so bad that it becomes a criminal offense, it's councils who order dogs to be put down, or recorded on some shameful watchlist. Something like the *Vicious Animal Register*.) 'You just do what you have to do,' I said. 'I mean it.'

'Oh, Markus, no – really, I'm fine,' she said. 'Please just get on with your day. I'll see you on Thursday in class.'

Just before we hung up, I promised to check in again on Wednesday to see how she was doing. The shock would have worn off by then and she'd have had some time to think about it. It would also give us all an idea if we should stay away that coming Thursday, or quite literally face the music.

Wednesday would be the truer reckoning.

I could feel it already then.

*

The ensuing days were also colossally wet.

It suited the mood.

I took the dogs out in the rain, and I watched their every move, and observed their dubious attributes – Reuben's unkempt hedges of fur, the grainy gold in his eyes. Then Archer's virtuous outlook, masking the villain within.

We walked through the woods of the park, and the mud. Their claws on roadside and grass. There was a definite looming darkness, of marches to gallows and justice. Shoes, legs, paws, snouts. All was soaked and stuck to us. The guilt hung low in the sky.

On Wednesday, I made the call at noon.

As I'd suspected, Lindi had now had time to fully absorb what had happened, and worse, what *might* have. She explained that once or twice she'd brought her daughter in with her, and the thought of those dogs rearing up on her was a different matter altogether. On top of that, there was the future to consider. A sweet-natured person like Lindi is always going to be more concerned about what might happen to someone else. She wasn't slighted for her own sake, but what if she let all this go and something terrible happened down the line, not so much to another person, but to another person's child? How could she live with herself then?

I told her again that if she needed to call the authorities, she should. I even mentioned the dreaded *council* word this time, and by Thursday afternoon, when we turned up for class (she insisted we still come), first at 3:30 for Noah, then 5:30 for Kitty, I walked in as if to an execution – especially seeing Lindi's arm, bandaged at the elbow. At the end of Noah's lesson, she grinned at me and said, 'Hey, you've gotta stop looking so sad! It's all going to be okay.' Unbelievable, I thought, she's rallied!

You have to know the mayhem at the changeover of those classes to understand that this was a ten-second exchange. It wasn't till the end of Kitty's class at 6:30, after which there were no more lessons, that we had a longer, final talk. Lindi said that while it had been one hell of an awful scare, and the dogs had come in hard, they'd also backed away. Without saying it, she was putting faith in what she thought of us as humans.

Misguided, you think?

Most likely.

And not because I consider us terrible people, but more just that we can't control every circumstance. Either way, it was pure relief, and more so, immeasurable gratitude. I still feel it now, almost eight years later.

As a last vote of thanks, and without going into the details, cards were written, gifts were given, but it would take some time to heal things. The first few months were tricky, especially dealing with the voices and the whispers, mostly in our own heads.

'They're the ones with the vicious dogs who bit Lindi . . .'

'How did those dogs not get put down?'

'Well, Lindi's a saint, that's how . . .'

And so on.

What helped was the tight-knit group of parents I'd become friends with in Kitty's class, including Andy, Lindi's brother-in-law. He rang me at some point to say that, sure, it was a bad thing that had happened, but not the end of the world. A child psychologist and not-so-in-the-closet comedian (he thinks he's hilarious), he deadpanned something along the lines of, 'Frankly, Lindi's such a painful person, this has been coming for quite some time.' He was calling from the Blue Mountains on a weekend family vacation – trying to make me laugh, and I did. What can I tell you? Sometimes people are beautiful.

As a postscript, Lindi and her family now have a dog of their own called Hamilton – and yes, he's a Cavoodle, but Lindi can have whatever dog she wants, damn it, and a Cavoodle is totally fine!

I also feel like time did restore us to excellent terms. Last summer, Kitty came home from the beach and said she'd seen Lindi there, and they gave each other a huge hug. It was quite a few years since Kitty had stopped lessons, and more again since you-know-what with the dogs. We were lucky, we *are* lucky, thanks to people like Lindi.

Which leaves us one more incident of horror, and I won't muck around, I'll get right to it.

This time, a year and a half went by.

There was nothing, no scrapes or scraps.

It was a period where the tarnished reputation was always there, but lives and goodwill went on.

In June 2017, we started renovating our house, and to get the job done we moved to a townhouse around the corner. It was down at the end of Woods Avenue, a small cul-de-sac, which we now just refer to as *Woods*.

Woods was a weird, rundown complex of tight three-level buildings behind a rattling driveway gate that only half closed, and that was when it closed at all. (It's still the same way now; I see it when I walk past with the Frost.) For a rental it was perfect. The owners accepted pets, and it was just rundown enough that we couldn't wreck it. We had a small sunny courtyard with sectioned-off grass, and the color scheme was gray carpet and terra-cotta tiling. It reminded me of the state high schools Mika and I went to – cold brickwork, steep stairways. Dark green handrails.

Given that moving house is much harder on cats than dogs, we cordoned off the kitchen, dining and courtyard areas specifically for Bijoux and Brutus. They could sun themselves and have both indoor and outdoor respite from Reuben and Archer, who would occasionally still corner Brutus. Bijoux was still the eternal enforcer, but new environments can change things. We thought we'd play it safe to begin with. The dogs were walked a minimum of twice a day, anyway, and usually stayed in my office. They didn't really need a yard, and with the strange layout of the place, there were other balconies they could utilize. Quite quickly, the cats were mostly in the sun of the copper-colored kitchen, with the dishwasher that sounded like a rocket launcher. It became the rule of that house. *Cats down here, dogs up there.*

Then came the start of spring.

Again, I was overseas, for just over a week.

(Before writing this chapter, I talked to Mika. I said, 'The first incident happened when I was away, and now this one, too . . . I don't want people to think I'm blaming you for things going wrong when I wasn't home – or worse, thinking you're bloody hopeless.'

She laughed. 'Well, it's called Three Wild Dogs *and the Truth*, isn't it? Two bad things happened while you were away. There were dozens of other trips where everything was fine. Not to mention, plenty of bad things happened while you were here, too. Just tell it like it was.'

So I will.)

Firstly, Mika was not to blame.

Sometimes, as they say, shit just happens, and this time, it all came down to one animal, one name, one indomitable personality. And it wasn't a wayward dog.

What can I say but *Bijoux*?

I was on another speaking trip in America, combined with a day or two going through edits on the finally finished *Bridge of Clay*.

One early morning, my phone rang but I didn't hear it. When I woke, I listened to an almost hysterical message from Kitty. All she said was that she wanted to talk to me. I sent Mika a text, and she assured me all was okay, and it could wait.

A few days later, I came home.

Again, it was morning, but this time brilliant sunshine.

I walked through the kitchen of Woods, out to the grass of the courtyard, and Mika spoke the immortal words.

'I think you'd better sit down.'

I closed my eyes.

Here we go again.

They were outdoor chairs from IKEA, painted black, and the yard was half in shade. I sat dead center in the dark patch. The metal was cold on my legs.

'What have they done?' I asked, each word its own mouthful of dread, and you know who I meant by *they* – and Mika just told me straight. Standing to my right, she said, quite simply:

'The dogs killed Bijoux.'

Just like that.

*

Now, consider how that feels. One moment you're sitting there, thinking, Geez, this chair's a bit cold, and then that gets laid on you.

'What?' I looked up sharply. '*How?*'

The early-morning phone call from a few days previous instantly made more sense. It wasn't an eleven-year-old girl having an argument with her mum, it was a kid who'd just witnessed a cat murder, at the hands of her own dogs. And just like the morning with Lindi, she couldn't quite tell which one.

See, Bijoux had been wanting the whole house since we got there. He wasn't satisfied with some lousy kitchen-courtyard district, oh no, he wanted it all. He was always shoving his head through the doorway near the stairs, where the dining area met the dog zone – and on a Saturday morning, when Mika and the kids were coming home from Noah's football game, Kitty opened that door, and Bijoux seized his chance.

As he sprang ahead, up through the tight turns of the stairs, the dogs were on their way down. They must have met each other blindsided, neither knowing who was who, and *BANG* – one hit – and done. They'd struck some kind of pressure point.

The cat lay instantly dead.

In my mind's eye, I see that tough but good-looking animal in a lump, curled up, on the landing. It's the halfway mark of the stairwell, and cat, dull carpet and dogs. The girl is skinny and blond, with bruises on her shins from the playground, her hair in messy braids. Her face is awash; instant devastation. Her screams ring out through the house. The dogs creep instantly back.

From what Mika said, Reuben and Archer had obviously thought Bijoux was some foreign interloper, but once it was over and they'd recognized him, their faces were stony-silent. They wore looks of astonishment and remorse, or what I often think of as the *oh, shit* look. Surely there was no way out of this one.

I sat listening, head in hands now, to this gruesome-yet-unsurprising chain of events – our house, an animal gangland. Though I knew it immediately true, I found myself talking, quite stupidly.

'They *killed* him?'

'They killed him.'

No softening from Mika, no sugarcoating.

She gave it to me hard, point-blank.

It was a fact.

Our dogs had killed our cat.

I let that sink in for a moment, brutal and bizarre as it was. We'd finally hit the darkest depths of disaster, and it felt not only entirely plausible, but also somehow inevitable. That cold, hard IKEA chair, it grounded me to a truth I'd always known, more as the years passed by. This could only happen to us.

As for Bijoux, I know what you might be thinking, that he was such a demanding animal, he probably had it coming. Well, yes, but let me tell you. Living with his boorishness, the ninja attacks, and all that hard-arse meowing for fourteen years was one thing. Assassination was quite another. Things would certainly be a lot quieter from here on in, but that didn't mean I wanted him dead. And not to go out like *this*.

Or did I?

In both realistic and romantic ways, it was perfect. More than any of us, Bijoux was a warrior. He was tailor-made for Valhalla. It was probably the only way he *should* go out – by the sword – although preferably not from within. It was the inside-job part that was hardest to take. I mean, couldn't he have just fought some bloody Pitbull in a back alley somewhere and be done with it?

But no.

That wasn't Bijoux's style.

Not grand enough.

Not story enough.

He was always going to go out big, and it didn't get bigger than this.

As I slowly took it all in, asking how Kitty was, and Noah, and what Mika had done with the body (she'd opted for group cremation), I admit there was something else; I was also slightly relieved. At least this time no humans were maimed. No thoughts of final injections, or the threat of litigation. But still, how much more of this could we endure?

For weeks, I couldn't look at our dogs in quite the same way, as they came to me, both lovingly and shamefaced. There are all kinds of theories on the memory span of dogs, but believe me, they knew what they'd done.

It's strange how we all react to these types of events, too, and for me, I was partly just disappointed. I couldn't tell people anymore that we had two children, two cats and two dogs, and that the children were the easiest to deal with. Bijoux, the warrior cat, was gone, and until writing about it now, only a handful of people have ever known. Not even Paul, our vet, learned the details. Every time I looked at those hounds, they looked back, saying — We know, and we're sorry. While it's true they were two wild animals, neither was wilder than Bijoux. He was our meanest, gnarliest family member, and he garnered the most respect. I've tried many times to produce an epitaph for him, but I can never quite get past this one. He ushered death into our household in the only way he could.

BARBARIAN TO THE END.

part four

THE BODY
SNATCHERS

TWO DOG-SHOTS

Fast forward.
  Two snapshots.

The first one comes from August 8, 2019, somewhere near 4 a.m. There's black sky and a quiet city, and streetlights flying by. I'm screaming down the Eastern Motorway with a dying dog in the back of my car. He's been panting in toxic shock for far too long now, and with a sudden silence, and a stillness that signals the end, I see the lights where I need to turn, and I know the breathing has stopped.

I look to the mirror, and through the sound of all other sounds – the engine reduced to a mist – I shout. I roar at the body behind me, leaning back, still driving hard. The turnoff now missed, behind us.

'REUBEN! REUBEN, NO! DON'T YOU DIE ON ME, YOU'RE NOT DYING ON ME NOW! DON'T YOU DIE, YOU BASTARD!'

He gasps awake, the element of surprise, and everything happening in this terrible here and now pretty much sums up our entire ten-year relationship:

Me shouting at him, and Reuben lying there, most likely thinking — Jesus, I can't even die in peace.

Then, second – April 19, 2021.

It's the kitchen table and dinnertime.

We've just finished eating when the message comes through from Paul. We'd arranged that he would text me the blood results (maybe we both dreaded a phone call), and now they're here. The message tells me that they've found what's wrong with Archer. It's a rare leukemia, extremely fast. He's in deep trouble and he's going to die. Paul's words are sad and concerned. *Keep him close tonight.*

I pick up my plate and walk to the kitchen. In front of me is a big vertical window, and evening shining in. It's that perfect last light, of warmth among the trees, pressed to the sheet of glass.

'Have you heard from Paul?' Mika asks.

I nod, and there in that moment it happens. I have one of those imaginings we all see at certain times. All I can think about is the plate in my hand and hurling it through the window – the thrill of broken glass.

Maybe half an hour later, I'm in the shower, the water working me over. I'm caught in the quiet stampede.

I stand in the downpour and cry.

THE DOG WHO COLLAPSED
IN THE DARK

Believe it or not, after the fall of Bijoux in the spring of 2017, nothing happened for close to two years. We had dogs who became angelic. (Which, okay, in our case, translates to no fights, no murders, no aggravated assault.) It was like having normal pets.

Interestingly enough, they were made for this part of their lives. Sure, the best stories come from disruption, but the beauty of stability was amazing. There were awesome mornings in the park. Epic runs on beaches down south, in all their ragged glory – especially a wild stretch we knew well, of cliffsides and drops and sea pools. There's a beach I know like a runway, not a single other soul around. Just us and rawest water. Waves and tide, sand and headlands. Wild sprays, white foam like a wedding cake. Reuben would sprint at me, laughingly, his tongue like a fallen-out clock hand. Archie would circle around and put his head through the gap in my legs. I can still feel the fur of his dog's head, wet, and see the love and the trust in his eyes. I smell that smell. Sometimes even now, I rub my thumb across my fingers, knowing the salt and smudge of that dog. It feels like nothing else. Between the depths of our signature hellfire, like Bijoux and torrential pianos, these were the dogs no one knew. Their mornings and evenings not so much of greatness, but just, good.

And dare I say it, their love.

And their love wrapped up in mine.

I loved those dogs so much, and it came back to me in spades each day.

By October 2018, chapters began and ended.

We moved back home from Woods.

Kitty was finishing primary school.

Bridge of Clay was finally released, and it was proof that things don't always go to plan. For thirteen years, I'd fought for the world championship of myself writing that book, and it showed. Where *The Book Thief* was a tremendous effort that appeared to have been effortless, *Bridge of Clay* demanded dedication from its reader. Sure, it suited Clay, my protagonist, whose struggle was big and beautiful, but it couldn't suit absolutely everyone. It's much better than *The Book Thief* in many ways, and the people who love it are special to me. When we talk about it after a library or bookshop event, I'll say, 'It's not a book for weaklings,' and we'll trade a collegial smile. Which is not to say I think it's *that* hard going (it's not *Ulysses*, for Christ's sake!) but it's different, it's itself – and again, it bears reminding that books, like dogs, owe us nothing. It's worth it for having done it.

*

Through the last three months of 2018, I went on three book tours: America, England, and here at home. In 2019 I'd be going to India, Taiwan, New Zealand, twice to the UK, twice back to America, a combined trip to Croatia, Poland and Sweden, then China, Hong Kong and Mexico. There would also be festivals from Perth to Byron Bay and Sydney. Basically a year of travel, and I would pay for that carbon footprint.

That was the year we lost him.

Early in 2019, in the summer vacation, there was a swansong and none of us knew it. A Kitty and Reuben special.

We were down on the south coast, and it was close to evening at Washerwomans Beach. There was the shadow of eucalypts behind us, but the sun in sheets on the water. Kitty found an abandoned tennis ball. Earlier, Archer had made a small play for charging at another dog (okay, so they weren't angels *all the time*) and was well and truly in the bad books – meaning he was sitting there, right there, exactly one meter from my feet, not moving a muscle. Poor guy, he hadn't really done that much, but vigilance was always key. He had to watch on as Reuben and Kitty caroused through the water, all throws and laughter and calling. I still see the gait of their legs, those knee-lifts out of the ocean, dog and girl combined. Maybe it was just fated that way, to give Reuben and Kitty a last glimmering memory in the year he would finally break. They lit up the beach and water as much as the backwarding sun.

The months would fall away that year, like planes touching down from the sky. The writing on the wall came in July, on the coast again, when I was briefly there with the dogs, fixing some things in the house. Reuben, in a matter of hours, looked frail and suddenly listless, his legs instantaneously fragile, not certain to hold his weight. He didn't want to walk up the street.

Given there'd been no other signs of illness, the first thought is always ticks. I checked him. Nothing. But ticks are so hard to find, and sometimes in unseemly places. So again, I checked, and again, nothing, but he was deteriorating closer to evening. I decided to call the vet, and maybe they'd be able to find it.

I took him into Milton, and nothing unwanted was found. Not a tick, no other parasites. Chloe, a younger vet on Matt and Carrie's team, looked him over, saying, 'Oh boy, you're really unhappy, aren't you?' Reuben, who was usually so proud, lay his head to the side, quite dumbfounded, and there wasn't much more we could do. Just watch him, get him tested back home, and hope for the best. Among other things, she considered cancer. But to me that couldn't be possible. This was Reuben, after all; indestructible. Close to hitting ten years, he wasn't even that old. Or at least not old to us.

Once home, and tested, everything came up negative, but if there's one thing I've learned with our animals – and the deep dark mysteries of bloodwork – there are secrets as yet unrevealed.

Early in August, I drove up to Byron for the writers' festival, texting home each day to check on Reuben. He'd improved over the last month or so, and we thought he was almost back.

A few nights after my return, somewhere between two and three in the morning, Mika and I were woken.

There was an echo. A whimper in the darkness, followed by a thud to the floor.

Since moving back home from Woods, some things had changed, some hadn't. The dogs still slept in my office, their beds in diagonal corners, but my office was now down the hallway, closer to the stairs.

When we heard the noise, we leapt from bed simultaneously. We hurried to that room and hit the switch.

In the yellow light, we saw him.

There, in the middle of my office, Reuben lay splayed on the floorboards. His legs were taken from under him. He was frantic-eyed and panting. In front of him, Archer sat forward, watching. What else could he do?

I remember our voices, wavering.

'Reuby, *no*,' and, 'You're okay, Reub, I've got you.'

But we didn't have him.

We were lying.

For a long time, much longer than we should have, we figured out what to do. Mika sat with him, his head on her lap. She stroked the side of his face, her palm on those black-polished jowls. All Reuben could do was pant. He was dying in front of our eyes.

Given all our veterinary history, I know where all the clinics are. The place where Reuben had knee surgery was also equipped for emergencies, open twenty-four hours, and I knew they'd moved to Rosebery. I called while Mika sat with him.

The woman who answered seemed fairly uninterested. She didn't inspire much confidence, so Mika and I debated whether we should wait this out to see Paul. Each passing minute made that unthinkable. He wouldn't be open for another five hours, and Reuben would never make it. I was ready to carry him downstairs, but Mika wanted to slide him gently on a foam mattress, and that's what we ended up doing.

For a while, we sat at our front door. To the left was the entrance to the garage. My car was ready to go. Seats down, dog beds and blankets in the back.

Mika: 'We have to tell the kids.'

I lay back against the wall, eyes closed. No choice.

First, I went up to Kitty, and what was I going to say? As it turned out, simple and straight.

'Hey, kid.' I softly shook her. 'Kitty . . .' She woke up, knowing something was wrong, and I confirmed it. 'It's Reuben,' I said, 'he might be dying. You have to come and say goodbye.'

Writing about it does me in, really, and the edits, every time. I feel the salt shoveling through my eyes. I see her soundless shadow in the dark, navigating the house, making her way to her dog. He was Kitty's dog above everyone's.

Then, Noah.

It was Noah who couldn't control it. He was totally distraught. You know that sound, right before a child cries? It's that high-pitched, almost inaudible intake of breath – reaching for something but never quite getting hold of it, and the world falling down within them. As a parent, when you're on the end of that breath, you discover the meaning of helplessness. You feel it inside your chest. It's the sound of loss, unrescueable.

We made our way down, to where Kitty and Mika sat with him. There are terrible and poetic things in our lives, and so often they're one and the same.

Woken-up kids are beautiful.

Sinking dogs are tragic and golden.

They hugged him in the bleary light.

Everyone was crying.

Soon I picked him up.

I carried him into the garage.

I got him through the hatch of my car.

He lay like he so often had, on trips down south and else-where, only this time just him, no Archer, and he probably wouldn't come home.

But still, you have to hope –

I plowed through the empty streets.

We hit the Eastern Motorway.

I knew where I was going, but only vaguely, and it was somewhere near the Dacey Avenue turnoff when the dog in the back stopped breathing. The streetlights hit the wind-shield, then gone, torn off. One after another.

'REUBEN! DON'T YOU DIE, YOU BASTARD!'

I've mentioned already how it felt. A numbness. A car like a moving cave, or the chamber of Jonah's whale. I see it now as a great, soulless world out there, and us confined to us – this beast-of-a-wolf-of-a-dog and me, caught cold in the darkness of a car. He's dead, I thought, is he dead? He's stopped breathing. 'REUBEN! DON'T YOU DIE ON ME!'

But he wasn't dead, not yet.

Or he was and he'd come back to life – I heard him suck in valuable air – and we continued through the dark. Five minutes later, I pulled into the small car park in Rosebery, jumped out, ran at the door, and hit the bulbous green button. The night nurse appeared at the glass.

'My dog's dying,' I called to her, from the distance of maybe a meter. 'Can I bring him in?'

'Of course!'

I ran back, opened the hatch, lifted him out and lugged him as fast as humanly possible – and perfectly enough, I slammed his head really, *really* hard into the doorframe on the way in.

'Shit, sorry, Reub!'

If I hadn't been so distraught, I might have laughed.

Inside, I hurried him past counters and various apparatus. I placed him on a table and the vet got straight to work. I can't recall anymore what questions she asked, but it was more about keeping him alive long enough to see if they could find what was wrong, and then, if operating was even an option.

With the questions asked and answered, the vet – I remember her name was Erin – gave me a final glance. 'Do you want to say goodbye to him?'

I leaned down and kissed his cheek, halfway along the snout. 'I'll see you, Reub, love you, buddy – you'll be okay.' He had the eye of a child and a wild thing. The last part I'd said in a whisper.

As I left I could hear his panting.

I turned for one last look.

You never saw such windswept breathing, and his body so many colors, of dark, near black and browns – on fire in a sea of white.

LAST OF THE BODY SNATCHERS

He survived.

It was no surprise. That dog was almost unkillable.

But it was also a close-run thing.

As I sat in the waiting room, there was a young couple to my left. I remember the man having long hair, patches of beard, like he was into Skid Row or Guns N' Roses decades after the fact. The woman was neat and petite. Really, they were only kids.

'How you guys doing?' I asked.

'Oh, we're okay.'

I sat staring straight ahead, ashen-faced, sick from my head to my tailbone, not sure I could feel my legs.

'Geez, mate, are you okay?'

I looked over. 'Oh, not really. I'm pretty sure my dog's about to die.'

I went on to ask why they were there, and I can't for the life of me remember. I recall the dog was a fluffball, and the problem not a problem at all, when compared to impending death. But they were nice, so why be frustrated? Not all of us can bring in some blasted-to-bits mongrel version of a trampled charioteer. I'm sure their dog's still alive today, probably due to them not leaving things too late.

And Reuben?

The vet came out later.

She said he was hanging by a thread.

It was most likely cancer of the spleen, and a surgeon would call me in a few hours. For now, all I could do was go home and wait. I barely remember that drive home, but I imagine it as fairly barren. I recall it still being dark.

I talked to Mika in the kitchen, I hugged the kids. They'd gone back to bed all together, in Mika's and my bedroom, sleeping among the teariness. Not long after they were both at school, I got the call, which gave us two options.

One was to go in, grab the spleen, fix up whatever else had taken a hit, then see what the bloodwork said, cancerwise. That would remove the current problem, but not guarantee a life span. 'It could be a few months,' he said, 'but it could be a few years, if you're really lucky – but of course, no guarantees. Actually not that likely. And first he'll have to live through the operation.'

Option two was to leave him as he was, do the bloodwork, wait however long that took to come back, and see if it was worth operating.

I spoke clearly into the phone.

'Go in,' I said. 'Just fix him. I'll risk how long that buys us. If he dies he'll go down swinging.'

I knew that dog too well.

It would take a lot to kill him.

By 2:30 that afternoon, we knew.

By 3:30, we were eating ice cream.

When the kids came home, no one said hello. Kitty just said, 'Reuben?' Noah said, 'Is he alive?' There were great big sighs of relief.

I had a few other things to take care of, so I took Kitty, Noah and Kitty's friend Wynter along, and afterward we bought the ice creams down in Darlinghurst and ate them on a grubby street corner. Nothing could ever taste better. Reuben was going to live. Even if we didn't know how long.

Miraculously, he was ready for pickup just two afternoons later, and the whole delirious experience only set us back, as I've mentioned before, $11,897.65.

Yes, you read that correctly, both times.

Just short of twelve thousand dollars!

The specifics of the bill lasted more than three pages, and now Reuben wasn't only the two-dollar dog with two five-thousand-dollar knees, he was the dog we'd poured another crazy amount of money into, in the hope he'd live a while longer. That's one expensive gamble, but I'd have remortgaged the house if I had to.

When I drove in to collect him, the world felt slightly altered, like when you come back out from a movie; the place looked different in daylight. I paid, then waited, and soon they brought him out. It was like he'd been tortured in prison, or at the very least, a prison *movie*. Shaved. Beaten up.

Drawn down. Sunlight stirring in his eyes. Like they'd brought him straight from the hole. I almost expected tattoos.

I remember them calling me Dad.

'Come on, Reuben, where's your dad?'

When he loomed around the corner, I thought, This dog might just be the Minotaur, and I thought it with great affection. I crouched and he came to meet me, his head aloft on my shoulder.

'Hey, mate,' I said.

— I know.

Of course, I can't really tell you what his thoughts were. I just feel like that was Reuben's response to most things. This time it was — I know, pretty rough, huh?

'That is one tough dog,' the vet said. She had a glint in her eye and I nodded. Reuben looked at me, half-mohawked, and the funny thing was, it suited him. The more you tried to destroy this dog, the handsomer he got.

The following Tuesday, I flew to Edinburgh for barely four days, including travel. It was there in an upstairs café I got the details of Reuben's bloodwork, and the virulence of the cancer.

The room was uncomfortably warm.

He'd get three more months if he was lucky.

When you read that kind of news, it's a really long flight home.

But predictably, Reuben went right on being Reuben.

He recovered well from the operation. His fur was growing back. The first month he was looking strong, but

THREE WILD DOGS (AND THE TRUTH)

I still had a lot of travel ahead, and we needed him to hang on. The last thing I wanted for Mika and the kids was for everything to come undone while I was away.

As luck would have it, it was right before I left for another ten-city tour of America when Reuben had his first bad day. First stop was Seattle, one of my favorite places, and I landed to news from Mika. Reuben had hidden himself in the garden, the way animals do when they're preparing to die. Paul had made a house call. My first bookshop event was further north in Washington State, and I couldn't help but start it by just telling the truth. I said I might be a bit off tonight because I thought one of my dogs was dying at home without me. (Later, during the book signing, a minimum of half that audience told me their own dog stories – testament again to what these animals bring to our lives.)

But again, Reuben pulled through.

Maybe it was only a warm-up.

Mika sent me photos and they were some of the best she'd ever taken of him, like a bear at the top of our stairs. When I returned he was looking good again. He'd have six good days for every bad one, but that ratio was looking uncertain. I still had a few trips to go.

Which begs the lethal question of *when*? When do you take them in? When do you stop the pain forever?

We hit November, and again there were signs of shakiness, a weakening of Reuben's legs. But again he would always recover. There were more good days than bad.

It was right after I left for the short trip to Chengdu, in China, and Hong Kong, when Reuben took his final downturn, and it came, as it must, with some comedy.

*

On Saturday, November 9, Reuben went down to our yard but he tripped on the last few steps. After going to the toilet, he needed help making it back up, and the incident obviously scarred him. Mika noticed the greater struggle, and saw that fluid was building in his stomach. I was due to be home on Tuesday, and she thought he'd hold out, he'd make it. Unless totally impossible, she wanted me there, for both his sake and mine – to be taken to die by his master.

In the early hours of Sunday morning, though, Reuben needed another toilet break. Mika let him out on the porch, but he wouldn't negotiate the steps.

She tried to encourage him. 'Come on, Reuben, come,' but he remained motionless, unconvinced.

As she often did – because he was just that bit heavy and awkward for her to carry – Mika brought out the light-weight foam mattress again, and gently, *very* gently, she lowered him down the steps to the yard. Easier said than done, believe me.

When he was finished, he stood at the bottom of the steps again, expectant. Have you ever tried pulling a fairly hefty dog up even the smallest flight of steps on a soft, cheap mattress? (I mean, who hasn't?) First you have to keep him on the bloody thing. Then you have to find enough traction to negotiate each ledge. Meanwhile, and this is the best part, you also have to cope with the bewildered consternation on his face, as if — Really? This is your plan?

Needless to say, Mika, being the trooper she is, after a few close calls and much wrestling, managed to heave him back up, then ease him into the house. He didn't even get up from the mattress to return to his own bed. He was just too exhausted. It's fair to say it wore Mika out, too, as she slept on the couch to be near him. And her night was not quite over.

Just as she was drifting off to sleep again, torch lights appeared through our kitchen, followed by the sound of knocking. She walked to the vertical window, and her eyes were not deceiving her.

Is that, she thought – *the cops*?

It was.

A man and a woman.

'Could you open up please? We just need to ask a few questions.'

Essentially, our backyard can be seen from a pair of tall apartment blocks, and someone, in their infinite wisdom, had reported seeing *a dead body being dragged through the yard, up into the house.*

Mika stood in the doorway. Wearily.

She dropped her head.

A few more seconds and she laughed.

I'm sure the police wondered if it was her own special blend of murderous, deranged laughter, and probably had even greater concerns when she so willingly invited them in.

'Here,' she said bluntly, 'I'll show you.' Then, further along. 'It's our dog.'

With the lights now on and the police standing at the cusp of our living room, they saw Reuben laid glumly on the mattress.

'See that dog?' Mika said. '*Normally*, if you were standing here like this, there's a good chance he'd launch at you to protect me – but as you can see, he's in pretty bad shape. He needed the toilet and I had to help him back up the steps. I can't lift him so I dragged him on that mattress . . .'

The police were more than satisfied.

'Got it,' they said, 'we're sorry about this, but we have to check.'

To this day, we wonder who the caller was. No one ever said anything, or even left a note in our mailbox. I hope the police got back to them, or else I imagine them telling their friends, pointing down from their window: '*That's* the house of the body snatchers . . .'

It was all the proof we needed.

Reuben had had enough; it was time.

Mika booked him in.

There are certain dates in our memory.

Tuesday, November 12, 2019, is the day we had to lose Reuben.

People in Australia, but especially in Victoria and New South Wales, will remember that period for the permanent doom of the worst bushfires we'd ever witnessed, and we've witnessed quite a few. The sun was the only thing wet, smeared red in a specter of smoke.

When I landed that morning, Reuben was on a shaggy gray rug, near the back door. Normally he'd have come to meet me. Mika had told Kitty and Noah the night before, and they were both cried out already.

I remember them leaving for their day.

There's something about kids in school uniforms, especially first thing in the morning – all those endless possibilities. Their hair still stuck to their heads, still neat.

From memory, the sky actually cleared that day, and typically, it was hot. It would be interminably hot and dry like that for the longest of summers to come.

Reuben was booked in for eleven, so there were still a few hours of just seeing him, and knowing things, like his fur, and the bump on his snout near his nose. The barnacle-encrusted jowls. Legs like sticks of kindling. All those amalgamated browns.

The two resounding images I have, though, are firstly, an act of defiance, and second, just honest love.

Maybe around ten o'clock, Reuben decided he wanted to go outside, and as he often did, he trotted to the back flyscreen and nudged it open with his snout. It was very much a sentiment of — Fuck you, flyscreen, get out of the way. And this time he made it down, *and* all the way back up. He wasn't going out without pride.

As for the second, it's just Mika lying down with him on the rug, her body leaned in against his, her arm across his shoulder. I took several photos of the two of them, and there's a lot of pain and love; a lot of loss. I cherish those photos, for both of them.

We drove him down to Paul's, both sick but also relieved. It was definitely the right time, or maybe a few days late. Certainly not too early.

We parked round the back and I carried Reuben out of the car, but again he had his dignity.

I placed him down.

He looked at me and walked in.

And how do we describe a dog's death?

How do I do him justice?

There's a tendency to try too hard – to make beauty, to make poetry – when there's no need to try at all; it's all laid out before you. Best just to tell it simply.

Reuben being so heavy, Paul asked if we could do it on the floor, so we did, and he lay there, and Megan (one of Paul's brilliant nurses, who's unfailingly kind and soft-spoken) helped make sure all was ready. A few needles, a few tubes, and Mika and I beside him. Soon he was quite relaxed, our dog gone down, full calmness.

'I can probably give it to him now,' said Paul, and we said okay, and he started.

I recall there was quite a bit of gallows humor, from both Paul and me, even Mika. Paul knew how to take us. I'm sure I said something like, 'Well, at least life'll be a bit bloody easier now.' Paul, something like, 'I'll miss that *You know I could savage you right now and not even blink* look he used to give me . . .'

In the end, though, what can we do?

We sat and there was all that dog.

That *roughness.*

We take these animals in, often grudgingly, and all they do is love us (and, you know, all that other terrible stuff, like destroying book deliveries, attacking people, killing other animals, threatening your friends) – but that's *also* why they get under our skin. We realize that no one could love them like we do. A great friend of mine, Camilla (who's had some problem dogs herself), says that a pet dying is almost more devastating, because humans come and go – they have more connections, they're out more in the world, out in their own lives. But a pet is totally ours. They stay. Only we knew them best. Only we really understood them. Only we could forgive them. In Reuben terms, only we sat with him on the warm smoky floor when his heart beat its last. Only we dragged him down stairways, and up steps, on mattresses, and clocked his head on the doorframe at the emergency vet at four o'clock in the morning. Only we nursed him through two broken knees, and screamed at him not to die, in a car screaming through the city. And only we watched on, all those years before, as he slowed down his walking pace to match the girl who loved him –

Reuben was dead, between us.

Paul said quietly, 'He's gone.'

THE DOG WHO BECAME
A GENTLEMAN

We walked in from the garage.

Reuben was dead.

(For some reason I can never quite commit to *passed away*. We might say it out of respect, but somehow I've always preferred the idea that we live, we die, and we might as well say it like it is. There's respect in that as well.)

Either way, he was no longer with us.

That imposing personality.

No prowling through the house, or claws on the wooden stairs. No head on my lap while I worked, nudging me to say it was walk time, or, as Reuben probably articulated it — Come on, man, it's *me time*. Reuben knew what he deserved, skewed though his opinion might have been.

Archer heard us pull in. He stood in the front entrance.

'Archie,' I said, 'you've got big shoes to fill.'

I dropped and gave him a hug.

I guess that's how you start when you're down to a single dog.

He had a bemused expression on his face, which wasn't entirely unusual. Was he unsure about another of Reuben's disappearing acts? Did he understand that this time he wasn't coming back? Did things smell different, were *we* different? I don't know. Again, much as I've committed the sin of pinning human thoughts onto animals (used everywhere from Hollywood movies to master storytellers like Tobias Wolff), how can we really know? We like to think they'll miss whoever leaves first, like Rocky missed Tyja all those years ago – but as we know, not all dogs are the same, and they react in assorted ways. I'm sure Archie did miss Reuben, but he was likely also wondering how long till dinner.

Mika went up immediately to get changed.

There was a good reason for that.

Before we'd left Paul's surgery, I didn't like the idea of leaving Reuben on the floor. He was suddenly so sad and flaccid, and just *damaged*. To the untrained eye, he could have been something forgotten or discarded. True, he was hardly inconspicuous, but I didn't want someone to trip on him.

Paul said he and Megan would handle putting him on the table, but Mika and I helped instead, and the poor old dog began to empty. Urine splashed on Mika, who gave me the look.

'Told you we should have left him on the floor.'

'Shit,' I said, 'sorry, he's the gift that just keeps giving.'

From there, Reuben was cremated, and much as we had

plans to scatter the ashes at one of his favorite beaches, I kind of liked having him around. He's in a delicate mesh bag in a nice gray box, with a plaque bearing his name on the front. There might be some potpourri in there somewhere as well, and that's if it's Reuben at all. (I think most people are suspicious about the contents of what comes back from those places. I wonder what happened to Reuben's big metal knee parts, for example. Did they melt in the heat of the stove? It's also not lost on me that Reuben and potpourri make for a pretty incongruous combination.)

It didn't matter.

Nothing mattered.

We were down to Brutus and Archer.

Neither was to be underestimated.

It was strange walking Archie the day after the fact. We were out early and when we hit the park, he accelerated, hitting full stride, which he hadn't done in a while. He'd been restricted due to Reuben's illness, and now we walked quite far through Centennial. The weirdest part was remembering how, in healthier times, Reuben was always our front-runner. Always on task. He'd get cranky if Archer was lagging. There was a vanishing act up ahead of us.

It would be interesting to see how Archer would behave in general. I had my secret hopes, and a rarity, I was right:

For the rest of his life, Archie became a gentleman.

I missed Reuben terribly, we all did. He had such a rusty head. He could be so domineering! Those noises, *intergalactic*. I sensed when Archie looked for him, too, but the gang leader was gone forever. The two-dog mafia was broken. He mourned him but adapted to the new circumstance. Where once someone would enter our house and Archer would fire at the door as Reuben's first lieutenant, now there was no longer a need. We grew more and more certain that they'd operated on a simple system. At some point, Reuben must have given that clear and intimate directive for Archer to scare the bejesus out of anyone who arrived on the premises. Only in desperate situations (like the threat of trespassing piano teachers) would he become involved himself. More often than not, especially as time went on, Reuben hung back and let Archer take care of business; he had bigger things on his mind. But now that the king was dead, Archie could be more himself. A prince at heart, and a softie.

And that was how it was.

For the next sixteen months, Archer participated in our lives like he always had, but now as the only dog. I won't say he and Brutus became *friends* or anything, but hostilities were long forgotten, and Brutie was now an old man. He slept on our bed even longer than before, or concreted Mika to the couch. He still had a few good crimes up his sleeve, too – probably what he interpreted as merely roguish quirks, or eccentric misdemeanors – but frankly, no one likes a rug-pisser. Especially when the rug's brand-new. I was back on the job like I'd always been. Washing, soaking, finessing, then sniffing for traces of *the smell*.

Archie was my only buddy now, in dog terms. We walked through that summer together, in the breadth of smoke in the city, and the ash of the southern coastline – the photos like snaps of the moon. He sat in my office while I worked. Or played family games of Monopoly, sprawled out on his back. He lay in our yard like in years gone by, face to face with Noah. The two second borns. They looked so at ease, so together. At one point, he had a yellow, decaying tooth removed by Paul, and when I brought him home, he cried in my office when I left him to pick up Noah from football practice. Mika sent me a video: 'Listen to your sniveling dog!' But as we always did with our animals, I could tell she was just talking tough. Laughing, but melting within. His pain threshold wasn't quite Reuben's.

A favorite period was during the first lockdown in 2020, when he sat with me as I pulled down books from our giant bookshelves, then culled, and dusted and reordered. 'Come on, Archo,' I'd say. 'Come on, Bud, let's get to work,' and he'd come.

Later that same year, when my knee finally needed operating on – nearly a decade after Reuben damaged it in the park – Archie lay beside me next to the couch, while I read, or watched movies and football games. I especially recall reading *Night Train*, the collected stories of Thom Jones, and Archer's face leaning upward, watching. It had mostly been him who'd listened in while we read to our children, looking at the text and pictures. Now I can't think of *Night Train* without seeing Archer's imperturbable snout, or the contentment in his eyes. He was great to have around, and he followed wherever I went. A brother, a son. My sentinel.

As for his dealings with people, Archer was a much-changed man. Believe it or not, we could have visitors in the house. He would greet them! He'd even let them pat him. I remember my friend Gus coming over and rubbing his back in the kitchen. Chronic shedder that Archie was, Gus tried, quite amusingly, to pat the fur back down.

'Forget it,' I said, 'it's never-ending. It's like painting the Harbour Bridge. When you get to the end of brushing him, you go straight back to the beginning.'

Day after day, we made those comical climbs of the stairs, where I'd stop, and he'd stop. I'd start again, he'd start again. Always looking forward, always slightly guilty.

— What? he'd be asking. — I'm not doin' nothin'. Just walking here, that's all.

He could lie in the sun like no other dog.

He could soak the whole thing up.

Near the end of 2020, we lost Brutie the rampant purrer, the millstone on Mika's lap. His household urinating had become fiendish to the point of pathological. He also strug- gled intermittently with eating, so after the appropriately fraught discussions, we took the fated drive down to Paul.

It was a hard one for Mika, especially. She and that cat were almost literally joined at the hip. When he sat with her, his purring hit pigeon-pitch. Me, I had memories of my own: pulling him out of a drain near our first house, his whiskers strung back into a mustache; he and Bijoux walking with me through the bush down there, behaving more like dogs; holding him over my shoulder after a shower once, still shirtless, and feeling the pads of his paws – how careful he was not to scratch me. Removing him from my laptop so I could work. The list goes on and on. So often those cats were curled up together (usually on my pillow, goddamn it), and it was always Brutie who'd followed Bijoux, just as he'd done now, if somewhat less barbarically. As the saying goes, thank heavens for small mercies.

And so then, as they *also* say, there was one.

When we were down to only Archer, we thought he'd

last years longer. Apart from living on the streets as a pup and surviving a case of parvovirus, he'd never had any health problems. No injuries. Nothing to suggest that death would come so hard for him.

In January 2021, he started lagging on our ritual walks. The problem was that he'd always been slightly lazy, so I didn't give it too much thought. As time wore on, though, we became more worried. In February, I took him to Paul for a blood test, but nothing came up.

In the following months, he seemed to have steadied, and he could still move beautifully when he wanted to. Much as Shoeless Joe had put on a few pounds *but he could still hit*, Archer could be not quite the dog he was, but boy, that dog could run.

As we all know of that year, COVID was ramping up again, but here in Sydney, full lockdown didn't hit till June. In mid-April, we returned from an afternoon at one of the kids' modified sports events to find Archie at the top of the stairs. Noah was up ahead, calling out to him, and I heard him say, 'Woah, Archie –' Then immediately to the rest of us, 'Hey, someone help!'

I saw Noah bracing himself, ready to catch him if he toppled. The dog looked dazed; he was swaying. There was clearly something wrong. Next morning I checked his bed. It was wet.

Everything was confirmed when I took him back down to Paul. First, Archie didn't jump in my car, where usually he vaulted in off a short run, or even no run at all. Then, when I had to park quite far from Paul's surgery, he wouldn't walk. I carried him past the dress shops, Sonoma Bakery, and the real estate agent, around to Paul's small shopfront – and that night was the night in question.

Don't ask me why the blood results came back so fast, but they did, and it was the moment of the kitchen table, and the imagined plate through the window. And the breakdown in the shower. I thought, Not Archer, come on, not Archie. He was only just getting started, he'd become such a gentle soul.

But as we know, in death there is no bargaining.

I slept that night on the couch, with Archie on his bed beside me.

In the morning, the kids said goodbye to him, and he was silently, awfully unwell. What was killing him clearly killed fast, but we still weren't sure what to do. Should the kids say their *final* goodbyes?

By about 9:30, we knew.

The earliest we could book him in for with Paul was three o'clock, but by ten he was really suffering. He teetered on the steps out the back – I caught him in my arms. He lay with his head in my hands.

I called again and talked to Paul's other great veterinary nurse, Phil, and after years of making the effort to be unfailingly easygoing, now was the day to abandon it. I said, 'Phil, this dog is dying in front of me, he's really suffering. Is there a chance I can bring him in earlier?' (I know, downright hostile!)

He was booked back in for midday.

In the meantime, Mika picked up Kitty and Noah from school. Halina was in the area and dropped in. Our good friend, and always friend to our dogs, Angus, was driving home from work at the airport, and he dropped in as well. I'd never seen him so dejected.

As you might have guessed, though, it was nothing

compared to Kitty and Noah. I'd seen them cry, but never like this. (Remember, I was still in Hong Kong when they were told they were losing Reuben.) Our new neighbors, who had three dogs of their own, commented a few days later that they could hear it. It was nothing if not visceral.

At midday, I carried him in.

There was no room in the back for us to park, so Mika dropped me off and I held him. Phil opened the door and helped me in, and it's funny, our gallantry through laughter. I don't remember anymore what was said, but I recall making jokes, likely complaints about Archie's weight, as I thanked them for taking him early. Our dog looked almost bloodless.

And the rest? It's hard to write it.

I will myself, machine-like.

This time we used the table.

Mika and I both hugged him.

I said, 'Archie, Archerboy, you're beautiful,' because he was. I told him the pain would soon be over, and he lay and he looked at me and he loved me. I'm not sure Reuben even loved me like Archie did, and maybe the truth goes both ways – for they know us like no one else does, and they forgive us better than humans. Their histories are deceptively complex. If Archie were human he'd have been a jewel thief. He pulled off the greatest culinary heists of our time. Or else he'd have been a therapist . . . In a final moment of clarity, I saw him outsprinting Reuben on the beach.

Within seconds, the fluid went in, so green, the trigger now limp in Paul's fist.

Archie's lips.

They'd gone so white. He was pale to pure anemic.

He lay restful now on the table, in death as he was in life – blond and positively handsome. His eyes gone gray and glassy.

It was just as I said in the prologue, like the tide had come in and taken him.

Archie, we more than loved you.

I imagine you out at sea.

THE DOGLESS DROUGHT
OF 2021

It hit me hardest next morning, waking up to a dogless life. No Reuben, no Arch.

They were gone and the house felt empty, because it was, in one specific way. Empty of all animals. Just us. All us arguing humans.

I made coffee and brought it back to bed.

I lay with my head on Mika, reminiscent of Archie on Reuben. It was then that I fully broke. I wanted nothing but to have those dogs back, who'd given us so much life, and caused us so much trouble.

The biggest difference this time around was that while Reuben dying was a seismic loss, we'd still had Archer; there was a need. He needed to be fed, walked and loved. Not to mention, we still had a dog to complain about – also incredibly important. If nothing else, we could marvel at his infamous shedding. 'Jesus, take a look. We could make a second dog out of all this, I reckon . . .' He forced us to hold our end up, and now he'd been taken as well, and something had died in all of us.

As weeks passed and we adjusted to pet-free living, Mika said I should write about the dogs while it was all still fresh in my memory (which she'd also suggested when Reuben died). Having lived with a writer who'd spent thirteen years on his previous book, I think she hoped I might write something quickly. Not for financial or aspirational reasons, but because writers are supposed to produce – to start books and sometimes finish them. But she also knew what it meant to me. What *they* meant.

'Those two dogs,' she said, and she was framed in my office doorway. 'They were such a big part of *you*.'

And, honestly, I promise, I tried.

I'd already written a few short pages over six or seven attempts after we lost Reuben, beginning with that early morning when he collapsed on my office floor. It just didn't work, the tone was all wrong. How lazy can a guy be, you might ask? Giving up after a few lousy cracks? But it's like I said at the start – I know if I want to write it from the first sentence, and I didn't have it, not yet. I thought, Maybe I'm just not ready. Or maybe I liked keeping them inside me.

As usual, I was probably just afraid. So much of my writing life has consisted of primarily that emotion. Abject fear. And doubt, not only in my abilities, but in my willingness to see it through. I couldn't bear the thought of failing them. I couldn't fail those dogs.

So what did I do?

I went surfing.

I drove to Bondi and Maroubra and was out there just before dawn. In the mix of light and sea spray, I saw my family, and Reuben and Archer. I saw Bijoux, the feline

Genghis. And Brutie, the sweet-purring urinator. I remembered mornings when Reuben was sick and didn't feel like going out. Archie and I would walk over the footbridge, and someone would always ask, 'Hey, where's your other dog?'

'Oh, he's got cancer. He's doing okay, but some mornings he's just not up for it.'

They were always genuinely sad, those people. 'It's weird seeing you with only one dog,' they'd say, and we'd go our opposite ways. From the experience I've had with friends and various family, human cancer makes us angry; animal cancer just makes us sad.

And one more thing.

When you get down to having no dogs at all, no one asks you anything. You become unrecognizable. No longer who you were.

Which brings us now to the inevitable.

Yes.

We took in another dog.

According to my calculations, it was eighty-two days, just shy of three months, and I have to say, despite all my love and pining, what a beautiful few months they were!

Within that stretch, Sydney went back into more serious lockdown, and despite the cleaner house, and much more time for ourselves, we missed our animals hugely, and our kids were becoming itchy. They were children who spent a lot of time with our pets, especially the dogs, so we listened when they spoke on that subject – or, more accurately, we listened and then said no. The wounds left by dying pets are different for everyone. Some people go out right away and find a replacement, others take years, even decades.

Some can't bring themselves to do it again at all. As far as Mika and I were concerned, we felt like we'd been through enough. We made a point of enjoying the break. Not to mention our vacuum. With all the dog and cat hair gone, that poor bugger could have gone to the Bahamas.

But you know what it's like, in the end it's always the same. The spark becomes a light, the light becomes a flame. A fire becomes an inferno. On a whim one evening, you take just a momentary glance at a few dog rescue sites, and all those pleading eyes. You make a few mental notes. You admit your sins to your wife.

'Oh, shit,' she says, 'really? You listened to those bloody kids?'

'That's a good point. Since when has their advice ever held up?'

'Exactly!'

'And we'll just have all the same problems,' I say.

'Hard to go away – we'll never live overseas.'

'Like we were ever gonna do that anyway.'

'You never know!' She stops. 'I know.'

By mid-June, we tried adhering to a no-look policy, but neither of us could help it. There were several appropriately underdog-ish dogs around, all of whom were tempting. I remember one called Cookie – tan with small black tiger stripes – but she still didn't feel quite right.

I should probably explain here, even if it's stating the bleeding obvious, what Mika and I both look for in a dog, and why they come like a loaded gun. I know I said Mika has a knack for finding problem dogs, but I know I'm just as bad. We have no argument with people buying purebreds or designer breeds. (Really, they're the smart ones, and I honestly don't hate Cavoodles – I swear on my mother's name!) But someone has to take the mongrels, the rejected, the unloved. Again, none of that makes us special; we just can't seem to help ourselves. It's what we like. We roll the dice. And maybe, just maybe, we like the chaos.

That said, again I abandoned looking.

Any and all heat came off from our children, which is something I'll always appreciate. Their pester-power is zero. Their request was registered and left. They put up with homeschooling, getting on with their lives. Sometimes we all spoke about maybe stepping up again, but the conversations faded . . .

And then I saw him.

On the Sydney Dogs and Cats Home website, a new dog had appeared, and he was a pound dog extraordinaire.

Big enough.

Rough enough.

Friendly looking.

Close enough to the right age (he was a year and a half, and we were looking for two years or above).

Actually, he looked like the sort of dog you'd find in a movie or sitcom, who mucks up but somehow charmingly, like running through the house in the middle of being washed, and shaking himself off in the kitchen. *That* kind of dog.

So I watched.

Here and there, I'd do some work on a new and supposedly small novel I was considering (it wasn't going well), then reverted to checking the website, and therefore, the dog.

He was still there.

So far, I'd kept him to myself – this white-furred, funny-looking thing peering amiably out of the screen. (Jesus, that pound's photographer – an absolute bloody Rembrandt!)

Till it was Friday afternoon.

July 9, 2021.

The dog onscreen, named FROSTY.

What a crazy name, but it suited him. Oh, and another thing. The small but glowing report did mention that someone with a bit of experience with bigger dogs would be ideal, just to iron out a few little habits . . . But he was otherwise friendly, gregarious, and *loves other dogs and people.*

So, you know, send in the numbskull, *muchas gracias,* sign me up!

I could feel the onset of excitement, but also gravest doubts. How could we even contemplate such a thing?

I looked at my office floor.

No Reub, no resting Archie.

It's here in the writing I should do as I've done before, as almost every book, story and film does. Perfectly enough, as a kid, the first time I recognized it was in a Tom Hanks movie, *Turner and Hooch* (a dog story), where the ending mirrors its beginning. It's how we trigger emotion, circling back to those signals of memory. In that movie, after Hooch has died heroically, saving the Hanks character's life, we fast-forward to see a replacement, a pup, being lectured not to drink out of the toilet – exactly how it happened at the start . . .

So this is where I could go there, to that moment, where this time it's my turn to call out to Mika, and for her to be suspicious and doubtful.

I should notice all the details:

A last strand of Archie fur in the light on my office floor, or the lingering scent of Bijoux, or Brutie.

I should call down to Mika that I think I found us a dog, and she should go, 'Sorry? What was that? I couldn't quite hear you . . .'

I'm not going to do that here, though, because sometimes our biggest choices feel destined to have been from the start. In this case, I saw the dog. I could see him within our family of humans and the ghosts of animals. When I talked to Mika, she already knew. Our kids – faced now with the prospect of it actually happening – were wary, and strangely quiet. Noah was more excited. Kitty was afraid, I think, that she couldn't love any dog as much as she loved Reuben or Archie. But it only took three or four minutes; she stopped, she said she was ready. We agreed and all committed.

I made the phone call that same Friday.

On Monday, we met a wild dog.

And then, despite *everything* – common sense, experience, self-preservation – we did what Zusaks seem to do in this life:

We met a wild dog and we kept him.

Our ride since then has been memorable.

(The last proof lies in wait, I assure you.)

Right now, as it stands, we've survived, and so, it would seem, has the neighborhood.

In March 2022, I started writing this book, eight months into having Frosty. As I finish the final edits, we've had him more than two and a half years.

In so many ways, he's exactly the dog we needed. He *is* friendly. He does love other dogs – well, most of them – and he would never hurt a person intentionally.

But he does demand an epilogue.

Make no mistake when I tell you.

Reuben might have been dangerous, and Archer his first lieutenant – and sure, there are thugs and saints of dogs out there, and everything in between. But somewhere in those grasslands, and the parks and beaches and cityscapes, there's a big white scruff-furred *running thing,* and out of all three dogs I've owned, whom I've loved and fought for, and both managed and *mis*managed, he's the wildest one of them all.

What the hell was I thinking?

epilogue

THE DOG WHO CAME IN
FROM THE COLD

His latest nickname is *Frozmoan*.

There's a reason for that, of course, which we'll stumble on soon enough.

In the meantime, I should confess that my first attempt at this epilogue was overly formal and philosophical, which wasn't quite right at best, and just plain weird at worst. When the literary figure you've quoted most in a book is Chewbacca, it seems a bit far-fetched to bring out the big guns in the final pages. I even mentioned Proust, would you believe, and his *vast structure of recollection* – so at one point I just said, Come on, man, just stop. No, it's much more in keeping with our story (and its creatures) to take my cues from the gut and the heart.

How to explain what's happened?

How to sum up how it's been?

Two words:

Goddamn and *Frosty*.

*

It's true what I said at the beginning.

This book owes its existence to him, for he showed me the way, he lit the path. He gave me the opening line, and that line is my first directive, of *this is how you write it.*

I needed disorder in the present to reflect the deeds of the past. The voice of heartbreak can be compelling, but what is it without calamity, without laughter and daily bread – the art of getting things done? I've learned to accept, or better, to embrace a world of all-of-it. On account of our many animals, we've lived a beautiful, brutal, awful, hilarious, escapadical life – and no, *escapadical* is not a real word, but I'll try to get away with it. As my friend, and once-owner of Edna the shivering Doberman, Tom McNeal, once said about the writing rule, *show, don't tell:*

'Yeah, don't worry about it – it's whatever you can get away with.'

A rule to write your life by.

And so what to do now with this third errant dog, and his creative knack for mischief? To be honest, I could have gone ahead and written another whole part about the wayward few years we've had him, but I thought I'd better spare you – and there's my loyalty to Reuben and Archer. They had to live their whole lives to get full parts dedicated to them, and Frosty's not getting anything without deserving it. I love him but I don't love him *that* much. (Actually, I love the hell out of him, but as Walter says in *The Big Lebowski* – a story of disturbances to the universe if ever there was one: 'There are rules here.' Just not show-don't-tell.)

So here, I'm just going to tell you.

The following is a fairly comprehensive list of Frosty's

THREE WILD DOGS (AND THE TRUTH)

dubious achievements so far. In truth, there are many more (it's been a bit of a blur) but if nothing else, this gives you a good taste of Frosty's contribution to the world. It hasn't always been pretty.

1. Knocking me over in the park. (Body count, four. Injuries, miraculously nil.)

2. Shit-eating combined with rolling in human waste, also in the park. (Disgust levels: extreme. My swearing and blasphemy gauge: off the charts.)

3. Harassment of people with those ball-thrower things. (Has now broken this habit, but there's always the chance of a brain snap.)

4. The vicious knee-shin-and-quadriceps attacks. (As seen in prologue. Final details to come.)

5. Jumping into the front seat of my car and grinning crazily at the steering wheel if I left him alone in there for even three seconds. (Also now under control.)

6. Never starting fights with other dogs but being bullishly determined to *finish* them. (Just ask a German Shepherd named Turbo and a certain nasty Red Heeler about that. It would appear that if you start a stink with Frosty, he's prepared to fight to the death.)

7. Sprinting after bikes. (Settling down now, but still needs to be watched.)

8. Horse-chasing near the track in Centennial. (Again, now under control, as are the next few entries.)

9. Motor scooter attacks. (Even while stationary at the lights, innocently idling, Frosty would go for the wheels.)

10. On the back of previous – wrapping me around a No Standing sign because a Vespa had just ridden by. (Memorable. Especially because Paul, our trusty vet, witnessed it on his morning coffee run.)

11. Vacuum cleaner attacks. (Once compulsive, now occasional.)

12. Lawnmower mauling. (Makes sense, considering.)

13. Attacking the lawnmower before you've even started it. (Those wheels, he can't resist!)

14. Severe harassment *every single morning* when I get up to walk him. (Never-ending – he jumps, he talks, he calls, he moans. He snaps. Honestly, I've never had such a talkative dog, or such a constant snapper. Those teeth come together like lightning strikes. He also has a yawn that morphs into accusation, as if — Jesus, could you move any bloody slower?

 And yes, I'm sure he swears and blasphemes.)

15. Chasing and hunting, combined with numerous stomping attempts at any flagrant, vagrant or variant of animal he deems huntable (which is all of them). Can happen anywhere, anytime, you name it, and it's hilarious yet unnerving.

16. Using his paws like hands, to curl around your legs and pull you where he wants you to be.

17. Using said paws to pull open a big, long gate on the south coast, to go after kangaroos. (As our friend Masami once said, after he sprinted past her, Angus and their dog, Busta: 'There was just this big white *blur*. It flew past us into the trees . . . *vanished*.')

18. Addictively launching himself over the aforementioned gate for more roo-chasing. (Once he knew he could clear it, there was no stopping him.)

19. Coming back from those trips impressively covered in grass stains, charcoal and dirt, and his chest slashed with claw marks – those scratches perfectly straight. (If they'd got him in the jugular, that's curtains.)

20. Returning from yet another of those excursions with a skin tag the size of a silver dollar – bright red, clearly ruptured by an upturned stick. (A sight to make you flinch. First I washed it with dishwashing liquid, but half an hour later I found some Betadine. When I dabbed it on him, he leapt up and roared like a monster out of the deep. No bite, no attack, just a shout, like — Man, that goddamn hurts!)

21. Attacking the nozzle of industrial-strength sprinklers on full blast. (There was no stopping that one. A whole parkland of people simply stood, watched, laughed and gasped. When he was done, his mouth was predictably raw and dripping blood.)

22. Really dining out on Dynamic Lifter in my mum and dad's garden, then throwing it up in my car. (Truly, sensationally repugnant.)

23. And most recent? Finding our gate ajar one morning and taking himself down to Paul's surgery for treats, when both Mika and I were out. (Very Frosty.)

And so on.

As you can probably tell, a lot of entries on Frosty's list could be chapters of their own. Consider the last one, which culminated in Paul giving me a beautiful little heart-to-heart about what a great job I've done with him.

'He came in, he was settled, he wasn't anxious in the slightest. He was so *wild* when you first brought him to us . . .'

Me? I thought. A good job? Are we talking about the same dog?

To top it all off, everyone we passed on our way home knew exactly who Frosty was, practically high-fiving him out on the streets. He'd obviously had a big morning, which perfectly sums him up. Much as I used to tell people that Reuben was a two-dollar dog with two five-thousand-dollar knees, or Archie was a terrible glutton, Frosty's calling card is easy – he's the friendliest but naughtiest dog we've ever had, by far. On the upside, he loves absolutely everyone, and he expects that they also love him. — Why wouldn't you? he seems to intimate. — I mean, look at me! (If only he knew that not only is he the naughtiest dog I've ever had, he's also the least photogenic.)

And then, of course, his other mercurial talent:

By God can that dog provoke me.

Even today, first thing this morning, I was delayed for some reason near the dog drawer (full of dog leashes, bog bags and tennis balls) and at one point I said, 'Hey, did you just bite me on the arse?' Mika laughed, as always. We both did. The madness and joy of the Frost.

'Good luck on your walk,' she said, as she often does, for there's always a chance I'll need it. So many things could happen out there. We are constant reoffenders.

... So what happened back in July 2021, when we went all-in again, applying to take Frosty from the Sydney Dogs and Cats Home – aka the pound, aka the group home? As always, it comes down to fate, because so many things could have thwarted us. First, someone got in before me, but that meeting didn't go too well. (Somehow, not surprising.) Second, we were informed with due diligence that Frosty had been returned to the facility *twice*, but also that he was a great dog, he really was! Third, given it was lockdown, they brought him to our place, rather than us going down to the pound. We were going to meet in the park, but they decided against that idea, and when we met him we realized why.

Kitty and Noah fell instantly in love with him, as we walked up our side path to the street, then walked him around the block. They loved the brown patches on his backside, and the splotches of spots on his ears. We ran our hands through the wiry fur. Yet his head and his ears were so soft.

All went well as his handler fed him cooked chicken on the walk, to keep him as focused as possible. I could sense how nervous she became when she sighted another dog. Phew. Frosty didn't see it.

When we made it back home, however, the real fireworks began. As pure coincidence would have it, our neighbors, Phil and Ann Maree, brought their trio of dogs out for a walk, and how do I put this mildly? Frosty went berserk on the street. Leaping-barking-flailing-biting-gnashing-launching-snapping – the whole shebang. Us humans were caught off guard, and there were shouts and cries and whispers, of 'Jesus!' and 'Shit!' and 'It's okay, I've got him – actually, no, I haven't!' It seemed to go on for minutes, and when it was done, the poor woman who brought him sank. We'd already agreed to take him, but she looked over, quite sheepish in the sun.

'So . . .' she began. 'Still want him?'

All eyes had fallen on me.

They knew it was me who'd do the work, me who'd be charged with training him. Me who would take any and all blame when there was anarchy like this on the streets.

I briefly studied my family, whom I knew would have sucked it up if the verdict was no. But there wasn't even the slightest notion of rejecting him. Again, that wayward belief. Again, the bleeding heart – the question of who else but us? I mean, who else *would* have taken Frosty after a performance like that? I'm not ridiculous enough to think we're the only ones, but I'm sure it's a low percentage. This was looking like hard work, but I couldn't just send him back. If there's one thing I can say about Mika and me and our children, it would be hard for us to quit on a dog. Not after even two minutes. I think the evidence speaks for itself.

When I said to Renee, the handler, that yes, we would still take him, she nearly buckled sideways.

'Really?' she said. 'I mean –' She cleared her throat. '*Really?*'

'We can iron that out,' I said, half reassuringly at best, knowing it would certainly be difficult, but never as difficult as it was. You saw what happened in the prologue. You know the first line of this book.

And so to finish that story for good now, yes, it's true, I admit it – I've had fights on the street with my dog. Three at least, and they were good ones.

To compound that, I'm certain that during the second fight, when Frosty assaulted my knees again, there was a young couple who'd seen the previous encounter, and they were stealing glimpses back at me. I was sure they were debating, whispering: 'Should we report that guy? He's abusing the hell out of that dog . . .' I recall they had a pure-bred Australian Shepherd – but soon the event we were working for.

One afternoon, a week or so later, we were on York Road, near Reuben's Field, and when Frosty saw another dog, he went for my knees and stopped. Abruptly, he sat, he looked up at me, and I showered him with pats and a hug. 'Frosty, good boy, you've done it! *You've done it!*'

Whether or not he'd have made it to that point anyway feels like useless speculation. The thing is, he was beating us up. It had to stop. We had a dog we had to stand up to, and the job fell to me, as it should.

So in some ways, Paul might have even been right.

Frosty doesn't pull uncontrollably anymore, he doesn't attack the person walking him. He doesn't wrap me around No Standing signs. He walks beside me quite serenely, the leash is slack between us.

Excitable? Absolutely.

Naughty as hell? On occasion.

Entitled? You wouldn't believe.

Hunting instincts? Palpable.

But you take the wins where you get them.

He listens, he tries really hard. We've narrowed down the hundred percent bad behaviors to five-percenters, down to one-percenters. When people come into our house, they're met with a friend for life. He flops on the floor for a pat, then laughs and moans with happiness. (The most recent nickname, Frozmoan, comes on the back of Frozmonian – as a play on the Smithsonian museums, but also his propensity to moan. While Reuben was a capable raconteur, he had nothing on Frosty for dialogue. Garrulous is the only word.)

As a sideshow, he'll sit on our kids' laps, legs outstretched, front paws cannily up – one of the more sizable lapdogs of the world. They call him Frozzle, or Frozman, and they'll kiss him on the snout, where his tufts hang wirily down. When he's bad we'll often threaten him: 'Any more of that and we'll cut off your tufts!' Once, when we talked about how we couldn't let him dominate us, Kitty said, 'Yeah, we're higher on the food chain – if we wanted to, we could eat him . . . Look, his jowls actually look quite meaty.'

Too much?

It's not.

Well, not in our household, anyway, as Noah then comes to his defense. He'd protect that dog with his life. 'No one's eating the Froz!' he'll say, or if not, it'll be some other nick-name. It's proof that families have their own languages, and the animals are part of the vocab.

As it stands now, we have a nearly four-year-old dog and he's a wildly spectacular soul. His face can be quite beautiful, just often not, as suggested, in photos. (He looks best midflight on a beach, all four legs off the sand.)

I've mentioned that new dogs feel like impostors early on, shaping up to the dogs of our memory. But deep down, I know it's more. I also say that I write my next book to atone for the sins of the last one, and I wonder if that applies here? Do I feel that way about Frosty? Am I atoning for Reuben and Archer? For all I got wrong before?

I'd like to answer yes, but the truth is – just like whatever the next book might be – I spend most of the time just hanging on, white-knuckled, for whatever control I can manage. That, and comparisons are pointless. Mostly, I love that he keeps Reuben and Archer near. Unforgettable as they were, it comes more readily thanks to the Frost. He's our dauntless, constant reminder.

But of course, Frosty's also just Frosty.

Someday he too will be a dog to live up to. He'll be the one we miss like the loss of a limb. He'll be the one we want near us again, in spirit – and so what can we do now but just love him, in all his joy and fury? (And swear about him, obviously.)

Sure, next time we'll be smarter. We'll make certain we don't find a troublemaker, a hunter, an escape artist, a fight-to-the-death-if-he's-picked-on breed . . .

But who am I really kidding?

Books begin where they end.

Maybe everything *is* circular after all – for if there's one thing I've come to learn about myself it's that I never really learn. That, and there's nothing like a dog. There's nothing like a dog who becomes both your conduit to the past and your wilderness in the present, and sometimes it bears repeating. It's their breath and fur and stink and eyes, it's how they rub up close against you. Knowing it, telling it.

— I'm yours.

It's all their disparate geometries; their angles of legs and ears, their warbles and gnarls, and how they always know what to listen for. Their anatomy – and more so, their spirit – hears many things, but at its center it listens for you. It almost makes up for everything. The deaths, the attacks, the cover-ups. Only a fool would do it again, in the face of these fast-moving histories. As I've said, regret, but never to change things . . . Okay, yes, I might change a few.

But not if it took them away from me.

The Frost is asleep beside me now as I write these final lines. True to form, he's snoring – a four-legged snowstorm. (What can I say, he lives hard, he rests hard.)

My computer screen is split in half: the left side is the writing side, the other half is Archie – sitting gentlemanly on the beach, an ear pointed out to the horizon. It's hard to say goodbye. Most memoirs make the same comment, that writing about the past just makes us miss everyone all the more. I miss Reuben and Archer every day. I miss Brutie, and even Bijoux, the warrior cat with attitude.

(And now Frosty is dreaming, motionless but sprinting, and talking his way through sleep.)

If you're ever in this neighborhood and you see a guy walking a wiry-furred, wide-eyed pound dog, feel free to call out hi. You probably won't recognize me, but you'll know me because of him. Also know that all might appear to be calm. We might be in total control. But that can all end in a heartbeat.

And you can bet that's what I'll write about: the vast structure of madness and mayhem, and the wonder of grudges and affection. If it's true that our lives flash before our eyes at the moment we die, I'm sure my dogs will be in that light. More so, if they're waiting on the other side? I'll know I'm not in heaven, but a place just left or right of it – some purgatory of love and chaos – and to be honest, I won't complain. I'll crouch and clench my eyes. I'll breathe and smell that smell.

I'll grab those necks of fur.

acknowledgments

Mika Zusak: the greatest.

Kitty and Noah Zusak: nearly as good. (Kidding – it's even-stevens.) Thank you for letting this book come to light. I know you're not keen on barely the smallest outside attention, but you let this one through. Huge gratitude.

Special thanks to Halina Drwecka.

Catherine Drayton, Fiona Inglis, Ingrid Ohlsson, Tracey Cheetham, Karen Rinaldi, Rachel Kambury: unwavering. Never forgotten.

Brianne Collins: mostly I think the only reason I write books is so I get to have you edit them. Pure joy (and semicolons). Thanks especially for turning a blind eye to my many deliberate wrongdoings, not least the capitalization of all dog breeds.

Grace Carter: many thanks for the photo-wrangling, and a few other good gets.

Cate Paterson and Erin Clarke: our books mean the world to me, but your friendship means more.

Dana Reinhardt, Laura and Tom McNeal, and Angus and Masami Hussey: always friends to us, and to our dogs.

Lindi Greenfield: talk about generosity. Everything I've said here is true. You really *are* the nicest person on Planet Earth.

Paul Hansen (plus Megan and Phil): thank you for supporting the very idea of this book, and especially for enduring Reuben's *I could savage you right now and not even blink* look. It's been a ride. Also, any mistaken veterinary details in here are my own.

Andy Greenfield, for constant reassurance and support . . . and your comedy, obviously. Thank you.

Melanie Kembrey: an article idea became a book idea. Thanks for your understanding.

Wesley Lonergan: big thanks for use of the Bijoux photo.

To the following people – never underestimate what you mean to me, and how much you help to accomplish all this nonsense: Praveen Naidoo, Katie Crawford, Judith Haut, Joan De Mayo, Nancy Siscoe, Noreen Herits, Kathy Dunn, Charlotte Ree, Andy, TW, TJW, JB, Raff, Gus, Clay, Scott M, Jane Turner, Green, and, as ever, Camilla Block.

Naturally, a few park people: thanks to Kate McDonald and David Staehli, and your memorably roguish dogs.

Cavoodle owners worldwide: I'm sorry. Truly. (I love you, I really do.)

Then last, and most: my guys. Reub, Arch, the Frost. What can I say? Love in the time of chaos. You gave me a book, and I never saw it coming. You'll be in that light for sure.

And, of course, writing is nothing without readers. Thanks to all of you who still fly the flag. It absolutely matters; it means the world.

mz

About the Author

MARKUS ZUSAK is the author of six novels, including *Bridge of Clay*, *I Am the Messenger*, and *The Book Thief*—one of the most loved books of the twenty-first century and a *New York Times* bestseller for more than a decade. His work has been translated into more than fifty languages and been awarded numerous honors around the world, ranging from literary prizes to bookseller and readers' choice awards. His books have also been adapted for film, television, and theater. He was born in Sydney and still lives there with his wife, two children, and the last dog standing in a once thriving household of animals. *Three Wild Dogs (and the Truth)* is his first book of nonfiction.